AN ANTHOLOGY OF BRITISH CUPS

Also by Michael Berthoud
H. & R. DANIEL 1822–1846
The first reference book to deal with this important nineteenth century factory,
provides a guide to recognizing the wares by key shapes and moulded borders,
illustrated with full colour and half-tone plates and line drawings.
ISBN 0 9507103 0 X

Further Publications
THE DANIEL TABLE WARE PATTERNS
by Michael Berthoud
IN SEARCH OF JAMES GILES
by Gerald Coke
AN ANTHOLOGY OF BRITISH TEAPOTS
by Michael Berthoud and Philip Miller

AN ANTHOLOGY OF BRITISH CUPS

by

MICHAEL BERTHOUD
F.R.I.C.S., F.S.V.A.

MICAWBER PUBLICATIONS
The Old Ship, High Street
Wingham, Kent

Published in 1982
by Micawber Publications
The Old Ship, High Street, Wingham, Kent
Printed in Great Britain
by Plymouth Web Offset Limited

ISBN 0 9507103 1 8

Contents

FOREWORD

A book on cup shapes and cup handles has long been needed. Many collectors acquire examples which on closer examination they find to be rather different from what they originally thought. A book in which apparently similar cups and handles are illustrated side by side, and the differences pointed out, will prove of value not only to the beginner by saving him or her from many errors, but to the experienced student or connoisseur by adding to his store of knowledge. Michael Berthoud's book is therefore more than a pictorial anthology of cups and handles, it is a copiously illustrated reference book covering a period in ceramic history, from approximately 1760 until 1860, which saw many changes in the manufacture of ceramic bodies as well as new developments in the evolution of style, from the Rococo through Neo-Classicism, Regency and Empire, Gothic and back to a Victorian version of the styles of curves and counter-curves that lacked the eighteenth century verve and sophistication.

During that period the attractive but technically unsatisfactory soft paste porcelains gave way to a hard paste which a number of factories in Staffordshire and the North Midlands manufactured, following the lead of New Hall, only to be superceded by bone china which still holds the field. These changes were accompanied by a great expansion of industry, many new factories springing up to take advantage of the new material and each developing a porcelain which either by paste, shape or decoration sought to capture a style-conscious but capricious market.

An immense variety of new cup shapes were produced often with complex handles and, as many of the wares were without identifying manufacturers' marks, many problems of identification have arisen. This book, by illustrating unidentified cups alongside known examples, should not only help to resolve some of them, but stimulate further research.

Michael Berthoud's well researched earlier book on the Daniel family filled worthily an important gap in our knowledge of early nineteenth century ceramic history. His new book provides a useful tool which most collectors will want to keep ready to hand for use. Much new material is included. Many problems will undoubtedly be solved with its aid.

Reginald Haggar.

ACKNOWLEDGEMENTS AND DEDICATION

I would like to record my grateful thanks to all those who have given so generously of their time and talents to help in making the preparation of this book a most pleasurable task and in particular my thanks are due to Sheila and Charles Barkman, Geoffrey and Alma Barnes, Joan Binns, Gus Brain, The Royal Museum Canterbury, Clive House Museum Shrewsbury, Jean Collyer, Robert Copeland, Bill Dickenson, the Dyson Perrins Museum Worcester, Nigel Gasper, Virginia Glenn, Geoffrey Godden, Ronnie Govier, W.J. Grant-Davidson, Reginald Haggar, Pat Halfpenny, Peter Helm, Robin Hildyard, Roy Hodges, Fred and Joy Hynds, Giulia Irving, Trixie Iwass, Liz Jackson, Mendl Jacobs, Joan Jones, A.E. 'Jimmy' Jones, Sir Leslie Joseph, H. McCall, John Mallet, Christopher May, Philip Miller, the Minton Museum, Arnold Mountford, Messrs. Phillips of Chester, Roger Pomfret, Betty Reed, Liane Richards, Royal Doulton Tableware Ltd., The Royal Institution of South Wales Swansea, Henry Sandon, Mona and Gerald Sattin, Jean Sewell, City Museum and Art Gallery Stoke-on-Trent, Alan Townsend, The Victoria and Albert Museum, Michael Wakely, the National Museum of Wales, Mrs. W. Warner and many others.

To all who can see in the simplest cups a glimpse of history and a fragment of our heritage and above all to the potters who created them I gratefully dedicate this book.

INTRODUCTORY NOTES

It is not simply to forestall criticism that I must begin by acknowledging that in preparing this book I undertook an impossible task. The project had its origins in my researches into the Daniel factories and their wares. The first, and often the most difficult problem, was to establish what was Daniel and what was not. Often there were recognizable links between one shape and another. Sometimes an intuitive leap was necessary and a speculative attribution could be arrived at leaving the connecting evidence to appear later. Fortune favours the prepared mind and time after time the awaited evidence turned up remarkably quickly. Having decided what could safely be ascribed to Daniel it then became necessary to explain why, for example, cups with closely similar handles did not qualify. In an attempt to do this in a limited way I included in 'H. & R. Daniel 1822-1846' three composite Plates, one showing Daniel cup handles, one showing similar handles used at other factories and one showing eight Etruscan shape cups. These three Plates evoked an amazing response and most of my correspondents seemed more interested in cups than in other wares. As a result I began photographing cups and given another five years could, perhaps, have begun to do justice to the subject.

My first intention was to illustrate nineteenth century cups only. The identification of eighteenth century wares cannot easily be demonstrated by means of photographs, so much depending on nuances of paste and decoration, the turning of foot rims and other minutiae requiring a knowledge of the subject far exceeding my own. However, it soon became apparent that 1800 was too arbitrary a starting date and would give a quite unbalanced picture. Gradually I included more cups from the eighteenth century but concentrated mainly on coffee cups as the handles provide a measure of help in identification which is lacking in tea bowls. I have not ignored these altogether but have included a selection (Plates 25-36) simply to give some idea of the range of shapes that may be found. The process of selection is a more or less arbitrary one, depending to some extent on the author's preferences and prejudice, and I hope that my natural bias towards the nineteenth rather than the eighteenth century, towards the products of Staffordshire and towards the decorated rather than the plain have not been over-indulged. That this is in no sense an encyclopedia is reflected in my deliberate choice of title —anthology:— a collection of flowers.

When a sufficiently large series of photographs are set out the gradual process of change becomes apparent, the earliest cups showing a surprising variety of mouldings and handle forms. These gradually give way to the simple straight sided coffee cups, mostly thrown and turned, with more or less plain loop handles, clearly appealing to a wider market and necessitating production on an ever-increasing scale. Towards the end of the century fresh mouldings appear, vertically reeded or shanked and fluted. These latter are mostly twisted from left to right, with certain exceptions which include Derby (Plates 121 and 125), Chelsea/Derby (Plate 122) Neale (Plates 123 and 124) and at least one other factory (Plate 126).

Another popular form was the vertically faceted cup called 'Hamilton Flute' at Derby but made by most factories (Plates 127-138).

By this time, c. 1800, the tea cup was becoming larger and the coffee cup had become a straight sided can. Most cans had completely vertical sides except for a few exceptions with a slightly narrowed base (Plates 250, 341 and 342) and tapered cans were fairly common (Plates 266, 268 and 276). These were mostly of equal height and diameter, contrary to appearance, with more variation in size than in proportion. The plain cup, called the Bute shape, with its accompanying can became universally popular until c. 1812, coinciding with the change from hard paste porcelain to bone china and providing ample plain surfaces for colourful, though often restrained, decoration in the Regency taste. The Worcester shape, with a pronounced break in the external curve (Plates 298, 303 and 305), the early French shape (Plates 247-258) and the porringer shape with flared lip (Plates 289, 295, 296, etc.) may be regarded as no more than variations in the basic Bute shape.

The introduction of the London shape c. 1812 was little short of revolutionary and this elegant shape (Plates 337-414) reigned supreme until c. 1822. It was not without rivals, particularly towards 1820, and during the same period mouldings once again made their appearance. London tea cups were usually accompanied by a matching, narrower coffee cup but a few factories produced a tea cup and matching can, notably Derby (Plates 337 and 338), Worcester (Plates 339 and 340) and Davenport (recorded by Cushion (12) page 150, but not illustrated here). Their production also coincided with a period when retailers generally prohibited the marking of wares other than with a pattern number. As the London shape was the last universally popular shape, made by every manufacturer from Josiah Spode to Frederick Peover and in continuous production for over a decade, we are left with a rich legacy of mysteries. The London shape alone provides material for research for several years to come and the large number of unidentified cups illustrated here is evidence of this.

And yet, despite the fact that few factory pattern books have survived from the dozens which must have been in use at any one time, many of the patterns themselves still exist, often marked with their appropriate number.

Unfortunately, as prices rise, whole services coming into the market are more often than not split up and sold as individual pieces. Many were marked only on one or two pieces and so the evidence becomes further diluted and scattered. The decade of the London shape presents difficulties because of the universal popularity of the shape, while the succeeding twenty years present even greater problems not only because of the proliferation of manufacturers, many of them probably on a quite modest scale, but from the diversity of shapes and designs and the sheer exuberance and ingenuity that followed when the aesthetic restraints of the Regency style were removed.

In attempting to identify unmarked pieces I have followed several basic assumptions, while acknowledging that they may not be either true or appropriate in all cases. I pass them on simply as a useful 'rule of thumb'. The first is that during the 1820's and 1830's, when moulds became universally used, manufacturers strove not only to copy each other's ideas and keep up with fashion but, at the same time, to preserve their own identity by deliberately incorporating slight differences in design. Secondly, that while they were not above stealing each other's ideas, they rarely appropriated actual moulds and therefore accidental differences also occur between the wares of one factory and another.

Thirdly, although moulds became damaged and eventually wore out, they were usually replaced from the original blocks and the differences and similarities were thus perpetuated within a given factory. Fourthly, that most manufacturers developed some sort of 'house style' that changed more gradually than the moulded shapes themselves and is often in evidence in a series of successive shapes.

Finally, that the use of pattern numbers for the identification of individual pieces is fraught with danger. Pattern numbers can be useful evidence where a series of shapes and patterns has already been built up on the basis of independent evidence and where the pattern numbers themselves follow a sympathetic sequence. Plates 695 and 696 illustrate an example of the possible pitfalls. The two cups are remarkably similar, as are their pattern numbers, but were almost certainly produced by two different factories.

In tracing the development of any nineteenth century factory it is almost always appropriate to use Spode as a yardstick. The factory was already in production by 1800 using a good quality bone china body, the wares were made in large quantities and are usually readily available for study and comparison, they are frequently marked and bear pattern numbers that follow a simple and logical numerical sequence. A glance at two Spode cups (Plates 216 and 693) will serve to illustrate, without labouring, the point. These two cups appear to have nothing whatever in common, no 'house style', no apparent links either in design or quality. But if the sequence of designs is followed step by step the gradual progression from the earlier to the later cup will become apparent. It is these sequences which are important, not single individual pieces.

The purpose of this book is to set out, as far as possible, the extent of our currently accepted knowledge of cups and their identity. The large number of unidentified cups illustrated will give some idea of the size of the remaining problem and if this book cannot provide the answers it can at least ask some of the questions. To define the problem is to take the first step towards solving it. Like many other newcomers to the study of English ceramics I started, some eight years ago, in the belief that the field had already been over-researched and that any piece of English porcelain should be identifiable from one of the standard reference books. Unfortunately, even in the case of some of the major factories this is far from true and many of the cups shown here have not, to my knowledge, been illustrated before (see, for example, the Minton cups in Plates 131, 199, 200 and 319). It would be as well, at this point, to take a brief look at some of the factories or groups of factories which can pose problems of identification.

The Minton Pattern Books

There has in the past been some confusion about the early pattern books, of which four have survived in the Minton archives. Fortunately these have been preserved in a fairly complete state and are now in the Minton Museum, Stoke-on-Trent, by whose courtesy it has been possible to compile the following notes.

The Minton factory produced porcelain during two separate periods, the first from an unknown date variously estimated at between 1799 and 1808 and ceasing in 1816. After an interval of eight years production began again in 1824. Two of the surviving pattern books relate to this first period when, as might be expected, cups were produced mainly in Bute and London shapes. I have often heard it said that a separate book was kept for patterns without gilding. There appears to be no evidence of this, but on simpler patterns the number is often followed by 'x'. Book I is undated and contains patterns from 1-146, each pattern illustrated in water colours in a straight band. There are two discrepancies in this book, pattern 145 is not illustrated and pattern 94 is shown in two different versions. Many of these patterns are fairly simple borders, with or without gilding.

Book II contains patterns in the range 147-948, but the sequence is far from complete with only twenty-two patterns recorded between 309 and 868. From pattern 868 to 948 the series is complete. Many of these patterns are quite elaborate and incorporate a considerable amount of gilding. Patterns 192, 206, 213 and 249 are variations of Spode's pattern 878.

These early Minton wares, bearing what I have called 'first series' pattern numbers from 1-948 are often marked with a version of the Sèvres mark in pale on-glaze enamel with the letter 'M' below and usually with the relevant pattern number. Often the Sèvres mark is omitted (usually on patterns below 200), in which case the pattern number may be marked in yellow, grey or brown (not blue) enamel and with or without the abbreviation 'N' or 'No'. The cups bearing these patterns are mainly of Bute shape with neatly potted ring handles (Plate 320) accompanied by a coffee can (Plate 321) or London shape tea and coffee cups with Grecian handles which may be either thick and lumpy or fine and graceful (Plates 342, 361 and 362). Moulded London cups will not be found as production had ceased before they had become fashionable. A few early patterns appear on shanked and fluted cups (Plate 319) and on what might be replacements for the wares of other factories (Plate 131).

Following a break of eight years the production of bone china was resumed in 1824 and the 'second series' pattern numbers, relating to this period, are contained in Book III on paper water marked 1823. The significance of this book has been largely overlooked in the past, probably because of the confusion introduced by a surviving shape book containing a record of the various shapes of tureens, teapots and cups and saucers produced. The book itself was probably compiled at a much later date, probably in the 1840's. The most important fact which emerges is that these shapes, although lettered from A-W, were not recorded in chronological order. A few examples will clearly illustrate this.

		Pattern Range	Plates
A	Low Blenheim	1500-2000	793-794
B	French	707-1164	620-621
C	Bath Embossed	623-647	703-704
E	Dresden Embossed	1170-2000	479
F	Essex Embossed	1347-1394	701-702
G	Berlin Embossed	830-1126	622
H	Cottage (depicted as London shape)	26-840	-
N	(no name)	159-600	473-474

No names are given for shapes N-W.

From this it would obviously be a simple matter to rearrange these shapes in their correct chronological sequence, which is confirmed in pattern book III. This book illustrates not just the patterns (as in books I and II) but the shape of cup on which the pattern appears. The first fourteen pages are missing, page 15 shows pattern 26 on a cup of traditional London shape (designated 'H, Cottage Shape' in the shape book). The first new shape illustrated is shown as 'N' in the shape book and bears pattern number 159, followed by a gadrooned cup 'K' (pattern 568) and the Bath Embossed shape 'C' (pattern 623). A ring handled Bute shape cup reappears with pattern 786 but the remainder are mainly embossed cups of the 1820s. This book contains approximately 1000 patterns.

It will be clear from the above that the 'second series' patterns from 1824 begin again at pattern number 1 and therefore from 1 to 948 there will be both a 'first series' and a 'second series' pattern, widely different in design and on quite different shapes. For example, 'first series' 159 is a simple key pattern on a ring handled Bute cup, 'second series' 159 appears on the shape 'N'; 'first series' 171 is a predominantly gilt pattern on a ring handled Bute cup, 'second series' 171 has a lilac ground and appears on shape 'N' (Plate 473).

In common with the wares of most factories during the 1820s Minton wares were usually marked with the pattern number only and it appears that the Sèvres mark was never used on wares bearing the 'second series' patterns which are mostly of distinctive moulded shapes peculiar to the Minton factory. The two problem areas are the 'first series' wares not bearing the Sèvres mark and the London shape cups which have no single handle type readily attributable to Minton and will be found bearing pattern numbers from both series. Paradoxically, those bearing low pattern numbers (under 200) are more likely to represent the 'second series' and those with high pattern numbers 600+ more likely to represent the latter end of the 'first series'.

Group 'A'

If Minton wares pose problems despite the wealth of documentary evidence that has survived, it is hardly surprising that large groups of contemporary wares have so far defied identification. Many of the cups produced by Spode, Minton, Davenport and Daniel in the 1820s and 1830s have no exact parallel elsewhere. We now come to a problem class of wares that frequently show only minor variations between the products of one factory and another.

Before looking for a likely factory of origin I grouped a number of these together in a sequence of pattern numbers and allocated these to an unidentified source which I called Factory 'A'. Gradually it became apparent that within that sequence were the products from at least two factories and, more recently, it has been possible to distinguish at least five factories within this group.

In the absence of any marked examples identifiction must be a slow and cautious process. These wares all date from the 1820s and 1830s and are often highly decorated. They usually bear simple, non-fractional pattern numbers of 1000 upwards. We must therefore look for several substantial factories, each of whom had produced approximately a thousand patterns by the 1820s. There is no shortage of likely candidates. Most wares of the 1820s are unmarked and this restriction must have applied equally to firms like Charles Bourne and Mayer & Newbold who had formerly used their initials as a mark. The comtemporary wares of William Adams have been described but not yet identified. The Ridgways made porcelain at both the Bell Works and Cauldon Place and only that of the latter factory has been identified. Simeon Shaw mentions Elijah Mayer and a potter called Simpkin as making superior porcelain in the 1820s. The works of Enoch Wood have so far remained a closed book as also have those of Hicks, Meigh & Johnson. Alcock patterns below 4000 have not been positively identified.

Certain close parallels in patterns, bordering on outright plagiarism, are evident between some Ridgway cups (see Plate 530) and an unidentified group (see Plate 519) and I strongly suspect that the latter emanated from the Bell Works, though at present I can offer no other evidence. Again without supporting evidence I suspect that the cups shown in Plates 649 and 650 are unmarked Mayer & Newbold wares. Factory 'B',represented by a single cup (Plate 708) now forms part of an expanded Group 'A'.

Group 'C'

This group contains the wares of a number of factories closely related in shape and design but varying from pattern number 22 (see Plate 567) to pattern numbers in the 2000 range on exactly contemporary shapes. The group therefore contains both established factories and some newcomers and thanks to a single documentary, though unmarked, piece we can ascribe an approximate date of 1840 to the cups shown in Plates 567, 568, 627-630 and 658.

The serving pieces associated with these cups are usually melon-shaped, flat-bottomed and standing on four moulded feet. It seems almost certain that Alcock represents one of the group (see Plates 627 and 628) but much further research remains to be done before the various strands can be separated.

W(xxx)

Wares bearing this impressed mark were formerly attributed to Enoch Wood but this theory has in recent years fallen out of favour. Recent research carried out by Diana Darlington appears to support either Whitehead or Warburton as a likely manufacturer and an apparently unlikely candidate, William Adams, cannot be entirely eliminated. Some unmarked wares (Plates 298 and 311) may be tentatively attributed to this factory and a positive attribution may soon be possible.

Factories 'X, Y and Z'

I have not attempted to give a complete picture of this group and have been unable to illustrate any examples from Factory Y. Research is continuing and it is likely that the identity of Factory Z will soon be established, and that Factories X and Y will prove to represent more than two factories.

Some Questions

Why is the cup shown in Plate 524 fairly common but always bearing the same pattern, number 2802, and why do other patterns not appear on cups of a similar shape? Why are Daniel's Shrewsbury shape cups so common while jugs and teapots are comparatively rare? Why are the cups shown in Plates 651 and 652 quite commonly found with pattern numbers from 1100 to 1500 but with serving pieces so far not recorded? Which Staffordshire potter made the cups shown in Plates 653 and 654 in an exact copy of a contemporary Paris shape? Where was Joseph Mongenot (William Adams' modeller at Greengates) working from 1800 until his return to Tunstall in 1812? Were the Brewer Brothers, Robert and John, not differentiated in the Derby pattern books because they never worked simultaneously at the Derby factory? If this is so, where was Robert Brewer working before his brother John's departure from Derby c. 1805?

These and other questions must for the time being remain unanswered. I would be delighted to hear from anyone who can throw some light on these problems or who wishes to publish the fruits of research, not necessarily in the form of a full length monograph.

Some Conventions

For the sake of brevity and to avoid ambiguity I have used a number of simple conventions in the captions that follow. 'Plate' refers to an illustration while 'plate' refers to a piece of flat ware. Where a pattern number is quoted in full as 'pattern number 123' this indicates that the pattern number is marked on the piece illustrated. 'Pattern 123' indicates that the piece is decorated with a pattern corresponding to 123 but that the actual number does not appear on the cup illustrated, although it may appear on a saucer or some other matching piece. 'Attributed to' indicates that I have accepted someone else's attribution, the words 'probably' or 'possibly' refer to my own attributions, neither of which can at present be verified. Published sources are numbered at the back of the book and references in the captions are limited to the author's name and appropriate number. In naming Hilditch cup shapes I have followed Helm (21). The reference to the 'curlicue bar' as a characteristic of many Alcock patterns is adopted from Dr. Geoffrey Barnes, the acknowledged authority on that factory.

Michael Berthoud
January, 1982.

Plate 1
COFFEE CUP. D. 3⅜in (86mm) Ht 2⁹⁄₁₆in (58mm).
Worcester, no mark, tapered cup with flared lip, ribbed with moulded cartouches decorated with landscapes in mauve monochrome and the crest on the Havers family. Complex scrolled handle. *R. Govier.*

Plate 2
COFFEE CUP. D. 2⁹⁄₁₆in (71mm) Ht 2⅝in (66mm).
Meissen, crossed swords mark, in blue, hard paste cup decorated in coloured enamels with a scene from the Italian Comedy and with solid gilt interior. Compare the complex handle with Plate 4 below. *The Royal Museum, Canterbury, Kent.*

Plate 3
COFFEE CUP. D 3in (76mm) Ht 3³⁄₁₆in (81mm).
Chelsea, red anchor mark, large wrythen moulded cup with moulded leaves at the base (compare Plates 121-125), enamelled flowers and green leaves round the base. The handle probably derived from Meissen (Plate 2). *The Royal Museum, Canterbury, Kent.*

Plate 4
COFFEE CUP. D 2⁵⁄₁₆in (58mm) Ht 2⅜in (60mm).
Chelsea, gold anchor mark, cup with flared rim, decorated with birds alternating with panels of dark blue ground colour. The handle derived from Meissen (Plate 2). *The Royal Museum, Canterbury, Kent.*

Plate 5
CHOCOLATE CUP. D 3⅛in (79mm) Ht 2⁹⁄₁₆in (58mm).
Att. St. Cloud c. 1760, marked with a bird in blue enamel, cup with a lid (not shown) decorated with a blue and gold border and enamelled fruit and flowers. The entwined handle was used contemporaneously at Sèvres and Worcester (Plate 6) and enjoyed a popular revival in England c. 1840-50 (Plates 817-834). *The Royal Museum, Canterbury, Kent.*

Plate 6
COFFEE CUP. D 2¾in (69mm) Ht 2⁷⁄₁₆in (71mm).
Worcester, Chinese seal mark in blue, scalloped edged cup with sixteen vertical facets, decorated with gilt flowers alternating with panels of dark blue. Entwined handle decorated with gilt dots in a manner typical of the Worcester factories. *Private Collection.*

Plate 7
COFFEE CUP. D 2¹⁄₁₆in (52mm) Ht 2¼in (56mm).
Worcester, no mark, octagonal cup c. 1760 with enamelled decoration of flowers and butterflies in Kakiemon style. *Private Collection.*

Plate 8
TEA BOWL. D 3in (76mm) Ht 1¹⁄₁₆in (42mm).
Worcester, no mark, c. 1760, twelve deeply concave facets, greenish soapstone body, decorated in enamels with the crane pattern. (See Sandon (1) Plate 8). *Dover Museum, Kent.*

Plate 9
TEA CUP. D 3⅜in (86mm) Ht 1¹³⁄₁₆in (46mm).
Worcester, Chinese seal mark in blue, shallow cup slightly scalloped with eighteen vertical facets, complex moulded handle, green enamelled flower pattern. *Michael Wakely.*

Plate 10
COFFEE CUP. D 2¾in (69mm) Ht 2⁵⁄₁₆in (58mm).
Pennington, Liverpool, no mark. Straight sided coffee cup, rather squat with plain loop handle, hand decorated in underglaze blue with a bird on a branch. *R. Govier.*

Plate 11
TEA CUP D 3⅛in (79mm) Ht 2¹³⁄₁₆in (71mm).
Meissen, crossed swords mark c. 1760, decorated with enamelled trailing flower sprays, the hoop handle with slightly scrolled 'tail'. Hard paste porcelain. *The Berthoud Collection.*

Plate 12
TEA CUP. D 3³⁄₁₆in (81mm) Ht 2in (50mm).
Worcester, Chinese seal mark in blue, c. 1760, decorated in enamel colours with the 'Wheatsheaf' Japan pattern, flowers alternating with panels of dark blue. (See Sandon (1) Plates 61a and 75). *Dover Museum, Kent.*

Plate 13
CAUDLE CUP. D 2⁷/₁₆in (61mm) Ht 2½in (63mm).
Bow, no mark, blanc-de-chine design with moulded prunus blossom and two handles. *Private Collection.*

Plate 14
COFFEE CUP. D 2⁷/₁₆in (61mm) Ht 2½in (63mm).
Bow, no mark, blanc-de-chine design with moulded prunus blossom and typical handle. c. 1755. *The Berthoud Collection.*

Plate 15
COFFEE CUP. D 2³/₁₆in (55mm) Ht 2³/₁₆in (55mm).
Bow, no mark, straight sided cup with twenty one scallops, hand decorated with underglaze blue flowers. *Private Collection.*

Plate 16
COFFEE CAN. D 2⁵/₁₆in (58mm) Ht 2⅜in (60mm).
Longton Hall, no mark, an early form of can with slightly spread base, decorated with enamelled flowers. Although also made at Bristol the can shape was not generally adopted until c. 1800 (Plates 174 et seq.) *City Museum and Art Gallery, Stoke-on-Trent.*

Plate 17
COFFEE CUP. D 2¼in (56mm) Ht 2⁵/₁₆in (58mm).
Problem class, no mark, called by Godden 'Baddeley-Littler' (See Godden (2) Collectors' Guide July 1979 p. 61, decorated with a chinoiserie pattern in underglaze blue, with large loop handle with feathered top. *City Museum & Art Gallery, Stoke-on-Trent.*

Plate 18
COFFEE CUP. D 2¼in (56mm) Ht 2½in (63mm).
Lowestoft, no mark, c. 1770 straight sided cup decorated with polychrome flowers by the 'tulip painter', and with a typical large handle. *R. Govier.*

Plate 19
TEA CUP. D 3⅛in (79mm) Ht 1¾in (19mm).
Bow, no mark c. 1760,pineapple moulded cup with hand painted underglaze blue decoration. *Private Collection.*

Plate 20
TEA CUP. D 3⁷⁄₁₆in (87mm) Ht 2in (50mm).
Bow, dagger and X mark c. 1770, pineapple moulded cup with green border. *Private Collection.*

Plate 21
TEA CUP. D 3⁷⁄₁₆in (87mm) Ht 2⅞in (72mm).
Liverpool, no mark, beautifully modelled cup with vertical ribs and sprays of leaves, decorated with a floral border in underglaze blue. *Philip Miller.*

Plate 22
TEA BOWL. D 3⅛in (79mm) Ht 1¹⁵⁄₁₆in (49mm).
Caughley, no mark, unusual floral moulded tea bowl with blue rim and an underglaze blue flower in the centre. *Godden Collection, Clive House Museum, Shrewsbury.*

Plate 23
COFFEE CUP. D 2⁷⁄₁₆in (61mm) Ht 2⁵⁄₁₆in (58mm).
Lowestoft, no mark, fluted cup with blue border and blue dashes at the handle junctions. *The Berthoud Collection.*

Plate 24
COFFEE CUP. D 2⁹⁄₁₆in (64mm) Ht 2¹³⁄₁₆in (71mm).
Derby, puce crown and baton mark c. 1782-1800, with reeded base and moulded swags, decorated with minimal gilding. *Doremy Antiques, Herne Bay.*

Plate 25
TEA BOWL. D 2¹⁵/₁₆in (74mm) Ht 2¹³/₁₆in (71mm).
Worcester, no mark, finely potted tea bowl with greenish translucency, transfer printed 'Milkmaid' pattern in black. *The Berthoud Collection.*

Plate 26
TEA BOWL. D 3¼in (82mm) Ht 2in (50mm).
Worcester, Flight period c. 1783-92, open crescent mark. Waisted and 'shanked' (spiral fluted) bowls were introduced c. 1795 and remained popular until some time after 1800 (Plates 107 to 112). Decorated in blue and gold. *The Berthoud Collection.*

Plate 27
TEA BOWL. D 2¹⁵/₁₆in (74mm) Ht 1¹⁵/₁₆in (49mm).
Minton, marked No 72 in yellow, thrown bowl in a good clear paste, finely potted, enamelled pattern or roses with brown leaves and dotted flower pattern. *The Berthoud Collection.*

Plate 28
TEA BOWL. D 3¼in (56mm) Ht 2in (50mm).
New Hall, no mark, very slightly flared lip with a palpable thickening of the glass round the lip (from being drained in an inverted position), decorated with pattern 195 with pink and mauve roses and a swag border inside. *The Berthoud Collection..*

Plate 29
TEA BOWL. D 3³/₁₆in (81mm) Ht 2in (50mm).
Caughley, no mark, moulded with a double vertical flute and scalloped edge. Decorated with gilding inside and out. *Mrs. M.W.M. Cronk Collection, Clive House Museum, Shrewsbury.*

Plate 30
TEA BOWL. D 3⅜in (86mm) Ht 2in (50mm).
Pinxton, marked P in red and pattern number 222, with twenty vertical facets and slightly scalloped edge, decorated with gilt rim and leaves. Vertical facet mouldings were roughly contemporary with shanked fluting c. 1795-1800. *Private Collection.*

Plate 31
TEA BOWL. D 3in (76mm) Ht 1¹³/₁₆in (46mm).
Chelsea-Derby, gold anchor/D mark, decorated with trailing enamelled flowers. *Micawber Antiques, Wingham, Kent.*

Plate 32
TEA BOWL. D 3⁹/₁₆in (90mm) Ht 2⅛in (53mm).
Liverpool, unmarked, thrown bowl with distinctive flared foot rim, decorated with a scene painted in black. *Philip Miller.*

Plate 33
TEA BOWL. D 3⅜in (86mm) Ht 2in (50mm).
Probably Factory Z (see Holgate (3)) of good quality, decorated with printed fruit and flowers in a gilt urn. *The Berthoud Collection.*

Plate 34
TEA BOWL. D 3¹⁵/₁₆in (100mm) Ht 2in (50mm).
Factory Z, unmarked but conforming to pattern 104, with typically flared rim decorated with a red line and gilt anthemion pattern. *The Berthoud Collection.*

Plate 35
HANDLELESS CUP. D 3⅛in (79mm) Ht 1¾in (44mm).
Coalport, incised crossed sword mark copying Meissen, c. 1830. Scallop edged cup (a twig handled version is also found), on three flower feet. Decorated with pink ground above with flowers in cartouches and yellow below with blue feet. Enamelled birds inside. Compare Daniel's flower footed cups (Plates 571 and 575), which are much more delicately potted. *Private Collection.*

Plate 36
TEA BOWL. D 3⁷/₁₆in (87mm) Ht 2¼in (56mm).
Ridgway, no mark, pattern number 2/915. Unusually late example of a handleless tea bowl, with embossed trellis moulding and asymmetrical cartouches. Decorated with a dark blue ground and gilding. See Plate 647. *City Museum and Art Gallery, Stoke-on-Trent.*

Plate 37
COFFEE CUP. D 2¼in (56mm) Ht 2⁷⁄₁₆in (61mm).
Worcester, Chinese seal mark in blue on the saucer, narrowing slightly towards the lip, scale blue ground with enamelled panels of figures, birds and insects and raised gilding. *The Royal Museum, Canterbury, Kent.*

Plate 38
COFFEE CUP. D 2⁵⁄₁₆in (74mm) Ht 2⅜in (60mm).
Bristol, marked + in blue, hard paste porcelain of unusually plain shape with large loop handle, decorated with enamelled meandering flower pattern. *Michael Wakely.*

Plate 39
COFFEE CUP. D 2⁹⁄₁₆in (58mm) Ht 2¼in (56mm).
Worcester, solid crescent mark in blue, straight sided cup with generous loop handle, printed 'Fence' pattern in underglaze blue. *The Berthoud Collection*

Plate 40
COFFEE CUP. D 2⁷⁄₁₆in (58mm) Ht 2⅜in (60mm).
Worcester, disguised numeral 8 mark in blue, the loop handle vertically fluted, decorated with a transfer printed underglaze blue chinoiserie pattern. *The Berthoud Collection.*

Plate 41
COFFEE CUP. D 2½in (63mm) Ht 2¼in (56mm).
Derby, no mark, the handle smaller than at Worcester, hand decorated in underglaze blue. *R. Govier.*

Plate 42
COFFEE CUP. D 2⁹⁄₁₆in (58mm) Ht 2½in (63mm).
Worcester, open crescent mark in blue, hand decorated with an underglaze blue floral pattern, the loop handle vertically grooved. *The Berthoud Collection.*

Plate 43
COFFEE CUP. D 2⅛in (53mm) Ht 2¼in (56mm).
Worcester, blue Chinese seal mark, decorated in blue and red with the 'Queen Charlotte' or 'Catherine Wheel' pattern. Compare Plate 44. *Private Colection.*

Plate 44
COFFEE CUP. D 2½in (63mm) Ht 2½in (63mm).
Bow, unmarked, copy of Worcester cup decorated with 'Queen Charlotte' pattern. Compare Plate 43. *Private Collection.*

Plate 45
COFFEE CUP. D 2⅜in (60mm) Ht 2⁷⁄₁₆in (61mm).
Liverpool, William Ball, no mark. Cup with flared lip, delicately potted, hand decorated in underglaze blue with Chinese figures in a landscape. Very small loop handle. *Private Collection.*

Plate 46
COFFEE CUP. D 2¼in (56mm) Ht 2½in (63mm).
Bristol, marked X21 in blue, hard paste cup decorated with enamelled flowers, well formed loop handle. *Private Collection.*

Plate 47
COFFEE CUP. D 2⅜in (60mm) Ht 2³⁄₁₆in (55mm)
Bow, marked 2 in blue, decorated in enamels with the popular 'Quail' pattern. *The Royal Museum, Canterbury, Kent.*

Plate 48
COFFEE CUP. D 2¹⁄₁₆in (52mm) Ht 2³⁄₁₆in (55mm).
Bow, dagger mark painted in blue, hand decorated in underglaze blue with Chinese figures. *The Royal Museum, Canterbury, Kent.*

Plate 49
COFFEE CUP. D 2⁷/₁₆in (61mm) Ht 2⁷/₁₆in (61mm).
Lowestoft, no mark, standard shape cup with 'ear' shaped handle, decorated with a Redgrave 'blue bomb' pattern in orange and blue. *Philip Miller.*

Plate 50
COFFEE CUP. D 2¹¹/₁₆in (68mm) Ht 2⁵/₁₆in (58mm).
Miles Mason, no mark, flattened porringer shaped cup with flared lip, decorated with a blue transfer printed Broseley pattern, the handle with characteristic Miles Mason thumb rest pointing towards the cup. *Private Collection.*

Plate 51
COFFEE CUP. D 1⅜in (35mm) Ht 2⅝in (41mm).
Worcester, hatched crescent mark in blue, cup of standard shape decorated with underglaze blue floral print, the handle in unusual form. *The Berthoud Collection.*

Plate 52
Custard Cup. D 2¼in (56mm) Ht 2½in (63mm).
Derby, blue crown mark c. 1770-82, squat barrel shaped cup with neatly potted handle, decorated with enamelled swags of flowers and a gilt border. *Private Collection.*

Plate 53
COFFEE CUP. D 2⅜in (60mm) Ht 2⅝in (66mm).
Liverpool, Pennington c. 1790, cup of standard shape with elaborate well formed handle, decorated with enamelled roses with a rust and green border inside. *Private Collection.*

Plate 54
COFFEE CUP. D 2⅞in (72mm) Ht 2¼in (56mm).
Factory unknown, possibly Enoch Wood c. 1800, no mark, bucket shaped cup with twenty four vertical facets, decorated with enamelled roses, elaborate two-spurred handle. *Private Collection.*

Plate 55
COFFEE CUP. D 2½in (63mm) Ht 3in (76mm).
Worcester, crossed swords mark and 9 in blue, a very tall cylindrical cup decorated with an inner gilt dontil border. *The Victoria and Albert Museum.*

Plate 56
COFFEE CUP. D 2¾in (69mm) Ht 3in (76mm).
Caughley, painted S mark in blue, cup of very large size, decorated with underglaze blue fruit and flowers, the loop handle vertically grooved. *Clive House Museum, Shrewsbury.*

Plate 57
COFFEE CUP. D 2⁷⁄₁₆in (61mm) Ht 2½in (63mm).
Caughley, printed S mark in blue, decorated with the underglaze blue 'Fence' pattern, the loop smaller and neater than at Worcester. Compare Plate 39. *The Berthoud Collection.*

Plate 58
COFFEE CUP. D 2³⁄₁₆in (55mm) Ht 2⅜in (60mm).
Caughley, printed C mark in blue, a small cup decorated with the 'Chinese Vase' pattern in underglaze blue. *The Berthoud Collection.*

Plate 59
COFFEE CUP. D 2⁵⁄₁₆in (58mm) Ht 2¾in (69mm).
Caughley, printed S mark, a very tall narrow cup decorated with the printed 'Fence and House' pattern in underglaze blue. *The Berthoud Collection.*

Plate 60
COFFEE CUP. D 2⁷⁄₁₆in (61mm) Ht 2½in (63mm).
New Hall, no mark, straight sided cup with pronounced footrim, possibly representing a development towards the straight sided can (Compare Plates 341 and 342), decorated in underglaze blue with the 'Java Village' or 'Mortar' pattern. *The Berthoud Collection.*

Plate 61
COFFEE CUP. D 2 3/16in (55mm) Ht 2 5/16in (58mm).
Lowestoft, no mark, standard shape and typical handle, with hand painted pattern in underglaze blue with blue dashes by the handle junctions. *The Berthoud Collection.*

Plate 62
COFFEE CUP. D 2 1/8in (53mm) Ht 2 1/2in (63mm).
Lowestoft, no mark, of standard shape with typical handle, decorated with enamelled flowers. *The Berthoud Collection.*

Plate 63
COFFEE CUP. D 2 3/8in (60mm) Ht 2 7/16in (61mm).
Caughley, marked S and X in blue. 'Royal Flute' shape, decorated with an underglaze blue transfer pattern, small pad joining the lower handle finial to the cup. *Clive House Museum, Shrewsbury.*

Plate 64
COFFEE CUP. D 2 3/8in (60mm) Ht 2 3/8in (60mm).
Bristol/Champion, no mark, decorated with green swags and with gilt border inside. *Michael Wakely.*

Plate 65
COFFEE CUP. D 2 3/4in (69mm) Ht 2 13/16in (71mm).
Worcester, crescent mark in blue, reeded moulding to the body, decorated with a pale blue band above and below and enamelled flowers. *The Royal Museum, Canterbury.*

Plate 66
COFFEE CUP. D 2 1/2in (63mm) Ht 2 9/16in (64mm).
Chelsea-Derby, gold anchor/D mark, decorated with enamelled flowers, the loop handle with distinct lower finial. *Private Collection.*

Plate 67
COFFEE CUP. D 2⁹⁄₁₆in (64mm) Ht 2½in (63mm).
Factory Z, marked No 54, (see Holgate (3)), decorated inside with a pink and gilt pattern, handle with thumb rest. *Philip Miller.*

Plate 68
COFFEE CUP. D 2⁹⁄₁₆in (64mm) Ht 2½in (63mm).
Att. Pinxton but probably Factory X, no mark, decorated with gilt sprays and dontil edge, handle with angled thumb rest. *City Museum & Art Gallery, Stoke-on-Trent.*

Plate 69
TEA CUP. D 3in (76mm) Ht 2½in (63mm).
Caughley, painted S mark in blue, an early form of the Bute shape cup with thumb rest handle and small pad joining the lower finial to the cup. Decorated with a blue band with gilding and white enamel spots *Private Collection.*

Plate 70
COFFEE CUP. D 2½in (63mm) ht 2⅜in (60mm).
Caughley, painted S mark, typical coffee cup accompanying the early Bute shape before the can became universal, decorated with blue border and gilding, the handle with joining pad and no thumb rest (Compare Plate 69). *Mrs. M.W.M. Cronk Collection, Clive House Museum, Shrewsbury.*

Plate 71
TEA CUP. D 3⁵⁄₁₆in (58mm) Ht 2¾in (56mm).
Factory Z, no mark, Bute shape with well formed kick handle, red line and gilt anthemion (pattern 104, Plate 34). See also Holgate (3) Plate 250. *Mercury Antiques.*

Plate 72
COFFEE CUP. D 2⁹⁄₁₆in (64mm) Ht 2⁷⁄₁₆in (61mm).
Factory Z, no mark, decorated with a bat print of a classical group in an oval panel, well formed handle with characteristic 'kick'. *Private Collection.*

Plate 73
COFFEE CUP. D 2¾in (69mm) Ht 2⅜in (60mm).
Factory X (see Holgate (3)), no mark, cup of good quality in a greenish translucent body, decorated with flowers in two shades of brown and gilding, unusual handle with ring and thumb rest, probably unique to this factory. *Christopher May*

Plate 74
COFFEE CUP. D 2⁷⁄₁₆in (61mm) Ht 2½in (63mm).
Possibly Coalport, no mark, well potted but with poor, orange/brown translucency, decorated with a brown flower and dotted leaf pattern inside, well formed handle with inner spur. *The Berthoud Collection.*

Plate 75
COFFEE CUP. D 2½in (63mm) Ht 2½in (63mm).
Chelsea-Derby, gold anchor/D mark, straight sided cup with loop handle decorated with black enamel swags, single flowers and gilding. *Jean Sewell Antiques.*

Plate 76
COFFEE CUP. D 2⅝in (66mm) Ht 2⁷⁄₁₆in (58mm).
New Hall, no mark, hard paste cup with slightly flared lip, decorated with pink and mauve roses conforming to pattern 241, with plain loop handle. *City Museum and Art Gallery, Stoke-on-Trent.*

Plate 77
COFFEE CUP. D 2¾in (69mm) Ht 2⅝in (66mm).
Derby, puce crown and baton mark, well modelled cup of simple shape with plain loop handle, decorated with a band of pale pink and gilt border. *The Berthoud Collection*

Plate 78
COFFEE CUP. D 2⅜in (60mm) Ht 2½in (63mm).
Caughley, no mark, cup of plain shape with loop handle, simply decorated with pink and green leaves and pink border inside, blue rim and ermine marks on the handle. *Clive House Museum, Shrewsbury.*

Plate 79
COFFEE CUP. D 3in (76mm) Ht 2⅜in (60mm).
Caughley, painted S mark in blue, rare bucket shaped cup with moulded basket edge, decorated with flowers painted in underglaze blue. (See Godden (4) Plate 51). *Godden Collection, Clive House Museum, Shrewsbury.*

Plate 80
COFFEE CUP. D 2,¹⁵⁄₁₆in (74mm) Ht 2½in (63mm).
Caughley, painted S mark, of similar shape to that shown in Plate 79 with less elaborate handle, decorated with flower sprays painted in underglaze blue. *Clive House Museum, Shrewsbury.*

Plate 81
COFFEE CUP. D 2⁹⁄₁₆in (64mm) Ht 2⅜in (60mm).
New Hall, no mark, hard paste cup with typical handle, decorated with green and gold swags. *Jean Sewell Antiques.*

Plate 82
COFFEE CUP. D 2¹¹⁄₁₆in (68mm) Ht 2½in (63mm).
New Hall, no mark, greyish hard paste cup, the handle following a line similar to that in Plate 81 but much less pronounced, decorated with the pink and mauve rose pattern 144. *Christopher May.*

Plate 83
COFFEE CUP. D 2⅝in (66mm) Ht 2⁹⁄₁₆in (64mm).
New Hall, no mark, standard hard paste cup with typical handle, decorated with an early transfer printed pattern in underglaze blue. *Jean Sewell Antiques.*

Plate 84
COFFEE CUP. D 2⅝in (66mm) Ht 2⅜in (60mm).
Factory X, marked 154 in puce, cup with twenty four shanked flutes rising from left to right, gilt decoration, the thumb rest rising to a point and not folded over in New Hall fashion. Compare Plate 83. *Philip Miller.*

Plate 85
TEA CUP. D 3,³/₁₆in (81mm) Ht 1⅝in (41mm).
Bristol, marked 5, hard paste cup with vertical fluting and wavy edge, typical handle, decorated with enamelled swags of flowers. *Dover Museum, Kent.*

Plate 86
COFFEE CUP. D 2¹⁵/₁₆in (74mm) Ht 2½in (63mm).
Bristol, no mark, hard paste slightly waisted cup with vertical fluting and typical handle, decorated with enamelled flowers and a blue ribbon pattern. *City Museum & Art Gallery, Stoke-on-Trent.*

Plate 87
TEA BOWL. D 3⅜in (60mm) Ht 2in (50mm).
Caughley, no mark, with twenty seven vertical flutes, decorated with a gilt border inside and a gilt flower in the centre. *Mrs. M.W.M. Cronk Collection, Clive House Museum, Shrewsbury.*

Plate 88
TEA CUP. D 3⅜in (60mm) Ht 2in (50mm).
Caughley, no mark, of similar form to that shown in Plate 87 with twenty seven vertical flutes but with typical deeply kicked handle, decorated with a blue border inside and gilding outside. *Mrs. M.W.M. Cronk Collection, Clive House Museum, Shrewsbury.*

Plate 89
TEA BOWL. D 3¼in (82mm) Ht 2¹/₁₆in (52mm).
Derby, puce crown and baton mark, bowl with twenty four vertical flutes and only slightly wavy edge, decorated with blue and pink harebells and gilding. *The Berthoud Collection.*

Plate 90
TEA CUP. D 3¹/₁₆in (78mm) Ht 1⅞in (48mm).
Worcester, open crescent mark in blue, twenty four softly moulded vertical reeds, handle with less pronounced kick than at Caughley (Compare Plate 88), decorated with a dark blue border, enamelled flowers and pale blue pebbled band at the base. *Jean Sewell Antiques.*

Plate 91
TEA CUP. D 3⁵⁄₁₆in (84mm) Ht 1⅞in (48mm).
New Hall, no mark, hard paste porcelain, rare shape with twenty four vertical flutes, decorated with a brown feather pattern 142 (see Holgate (3) Plate 37), with plain loop handle. *Private Collection.*

Plate 92
TEA CUP. D 2¾in (69mm) Ht 2⅛in (53mm).
New Hall, no mark, hard paste porcelain with twenty eight vertical flutes, decorated with a floral pattern 139, handle with upper spur (see Holgate (3) Plate 2). *City Museum & Art Gallery Stoke-on-Trent.*

Plate 93
TEA CUP. D 2⅞in (72mm) Ht 2³⁄₁₆in (55mm).
Chelsea-Derby, no mark, twenty four vertical flutes, rather coarsely potted handle, decorated with characteristic enamelled swags. *Private Collection.*

Plate 94
COFFEE CUP. D 2⁹⁄₁₆in (64mm) Ht 2⁹⁄₁₆in (64mm).
New Hall, no mark, hard paste cup with twenty eight vertical flutes and plain loop handle, decorated with the pink and mauve rose pattern 144. *The Berthoud Collection.*

Plate 95
COFFEE CUP. D 2½in (63mm) Ht 2⁷⁄₁₆in (61mm).
Possibly Neale, no mark, twenty five vertical flutes, gilt border and enamelled swags of flowers, Worcester type handle with inner spur touching the cup. *Private Collection.*

Plate 96
COFFEE CUP. D 2½in (63mm) Ht 2⁷⁄₁₆in (61mm).
Possibly Neale, no mark, twenty five vertical flutes, gilt border only, Worcester type handle with inner spur clearing the cup. *The Berthoud Collection.*

Plate 97
COFFEE CAN. D 2¹⁵/₁₆in (74mm) Ht 2¾in (69mm).
Sèvres, crossed Ls mark, *bleu du roi* ground with a classical scene in an oval panel and raised gilding, the kicked handle was copied at Pinxton and other factories. *The Royal Museum, Canterbury, Kent.*

Plate 98
COFFEE CAN. D 2¹⁵/₁₆in (74mm) Ht 2½in (63mm).
Pinxton, no mark, very slightly tapered can decorated in grey, green and gold, characteristic 'kicked' handle. *Private Collection.*

Plate 99
COFFEE CUP. D 2¹¹/₁₆in (68mm) Ht 2⅝in (66mm).
Caughley, no mark, twenty five vertical flutes, handle with fairly pronounced kick, gilt decoration inside. *Mrs. M.W.M. Cronk Collection, Clive House Museum, Shrewsbury.*

Plate 100
COFFEE CUP. D 2⅜in (60mm) Ht 2⅝in (66mm).
Caughley, no mark, twenty four vertical flutes and handle with much less pronounced 'kick' than in Plate 99, decorated with a pink border and blue cornflowers. *Bill Dickenson, Ironbridge.*

Plate 101
COFFEE CAN. D 2⅝in (66mm) Ht 2⅜in (60mm).
Derby, puce crown and baton mark, straight sided can with rope handle, decorated with the initials F.C. and arms of the Coleridge family (see Gilbert Bradley (5) Plate 258). *Private Collection.*

Plate 102
COFFEE CAN. D 3in (76mm) Ht 2¾in (69mm).
Bristol, marked in grey, large can in hard paste with an inverted 'ear' handle decorated with a green and gilt pattern. *Private Collection.*

Plate 103
TEA CUP. D 3³/₁₆in (81mm) Ht 2⁹/₁₆in (64mm).
Coalport, pattern number 6/237, cup of unusual design with twenty vertical flutes, slightly scalloped edge and very slightly kicked loop handle, decorated in blue and gold. *Bill Dickenson, Ironbridge.*

Plate 104
COFFEE CUP. D 2⅝in (66mm) Ht 2½in (63mm).
Caughley, painted S mark in blue, vertically fluted cup with sharply kicked handle, decorated with fruits painted in underglaze blue. *The Berthoud Collection.*

Plate 105
COFFEE CAN. D 2¾in (69mm) Ht 2½in (63mm).
Chamberlain, pattern number 193, straight sided bucket shaped cup probably representing an intermediate stage in the evolution from cup to can, twenty four vertical flutes, grey hybrid hard paste, decorated with gilt sprays. *The Dyson Perrins Museum, Worcester.*

Plate 106
COFFEE CAN. D 2¹⁵/₁₆in (74mm) Ht 2¹³/₁₆in (71mm).
Chamberlain, no mark, tapered bucket shaped can apparently peculiar to the Worcester factories, slightly kicked handle (compare Plates 103 and 104), decorated with a band of yellow and gilt borders above and below. *The Dyson Perrins Museum, Worcester.*

Plate 107
COFFEE CUP. D 2⅝in (66mm) Ht 2½in (63mm).
Chamberlain, no mark, tapered bucket shaped cup with twenty double shanked 'tramlines' rising from left to right (also used at Coalport, see Plate 108), greyish hybrid hard paste, decorated with brown flowers and gilt leaves. *The Berthoud Collection.*

Plate 108
COFFEE CAN. D 2¹¹/₁₆in (68mm) Ht 2½in (63mm).
Coalport, no mark, slightly tapered with twenty four double tramline shanks (compare Plate 107), loop handle with inner spur (compare Plates 115-118), decorated with a gilt rim only. *Liz Jackson.*

Plate 109
COFFEE CUP. D 3¾in (95mm) Ht 2¾in (69mm).
New Hall, no mark, slightly waisted hard paste cup, the blandly moulded shanking turning first to the left and then right, the finishing point being above the starting point, loop handle, decorated with a simple blue and gold border and blue flowers. *The Berthoud Collection*

Plate 110
COFFEE CUP. D 2¾in (69mm) Ht 2½in (63mm).
Factory unknown, no mark, slightly waisted cup with twenty four flutes shanked from left to right, loop handle with thumb rest, decorated with a blue and gold border inside and blue and gold flowers. *The Berthoud Collection.*

Plate 111
COFFEE CUP. D 2¾in (69mm) Ht 2⅝in (66mm).
Miles Mason, no mark, hard paste cup with twenty four flutes shanked from left to right, loop handle with typical thumb rest, decorated with a blue border and gilding. *The Haggar Collection, City Museum & Art Gallery, Stoke-on-Trent.*

Plate 112
COFFEE CUP. D 2⅝in (66mm) Ht 2⅝in (66mm).
Factory unknown, no mark, greyish hard paste waisted cup with twenty four flutes shanked from left to right, finely decorated with brown and pink flowers and gilt leaves, kicked loop handle grooved on either side. *The Berthoud Collection.*

Plate 113
COFFEE CUP. D 2½in (63mm) Ht 2⅝in (66mm).
Spode, printed mark, vertically fluted earthenware cup with sharply kicked handle vertically grooved on either side, decorated with a blue transfer printed 'Boy on a Buffalo' pattern. *Michael Wakely*

Plate 114
COFFEE CUP. D 2¹¹⁄₁₆in (68mm) Ht 2½in (63mm).
Miles Mason, no mark, 'Royal flute' cup in a barely translucent body, the handle with characteristic thumb rest, decorated with a blue transfer printed 'Broseley' pattern with gilt enrichment inside. *The Berthoud Collection.*

19

Plate 115
COFFEE CUP. D 2⅞in (72mm) Ht 2½in (63mm).
Worcester, Flight script mark in pink, waisted cup with twenty flutes, shanked from left to right, disproportionately large loop handle with large inner spur (compare Plates 117 and 118), decorated with pink flowers and gilt leaves. *The Berthoud Collection.*

Plate 116
COFFEE CUP. D 2⁹⁄₁₆in (64mm) Ht 2⅛in (53mm).
Worcester, no mark, similar waisted cup with twenty shanked flutes, large loop handle but with smaller inner spur (compare Plate 115), decorated with pink flowers and gilt leaves. *Micawber Antiques, Wingham, Kent.*

Plate 117
TEA CUP. D 3⁷⁄₁₆in (87mm) Ht 2¼in (56mm).
Coalport, no mark, slightly waisted cup with twenty four shanked flutes, decorated with a band of brown and gold leaves, the loop handle vertically grooved and with an inner spur. *Micawber Antiques, Wingham, Kent.*

Plate 118
COFFEE CUP. D 2¾in (69mm) Ht 2½in (63mm).
Coalport, no mark, waisted cup with twenty four sharply moulded flutes, shanked from left to right, loop handle verically grooved and with an inner spur, decorated with gilt lines only. *The Berthoud Collection.*

Plate 119
TEA BOWL. D 3½in (89mm) Ht 2¹⁄₁₆in (52mm).
Caughley, no mark, slightly waisted tea bowl with twenty flutes shanked from left to right, decorated with a floral wreath panel, blue and green border inside, gilt lines. *Clive House Museum, Shrewsbury.*

Plate 120
COFFEE CUP. D 2¹¹⁄₁₆in (68mm) T 2½in (63mm).
Caughley, no mark, matching coffee cup to the tea bowl shown in Plate 119 with plain loop handle. Coffee cups of this period were accompanied either by handled tea cups or by tea bowls of a similar shape and size, rather larger than their predecessors of the 1770's and 1780's. *Clive House Museum, Shrewsbury.*

Plate 121
COFFEE CUP. D 2½in (63mm) Ht 2⅜in (60mm).
Derby, blue crown and baton mark, sixteen flutes shanked from right to left alternating with moulded acanthus leaves, decorated with a blue border with enamelled flowers, plain loop handle. *Private Collection.*

Plate 122
COFFEE CUP. D 2½in (63mm) Ht 2⅝in (66mm).
Chelsea-Derby, gold anchor/D mark, moulded cup with leaves at the base following the shanking from right to left and with plain loop handle. Decorated with a blue border with enamelled flowers and gilding. *Dover Museum, Kent.*

Plate 123
TEA BOWL. D 3,⁷⁄₁₆in (87mm) Ht 2¹⁄₁₆in (52mm).
Neale, marked P in gold inside the foot rim, eighteen flutes shanked from right to left alternating with acanthus leaves (compare Plate 125), gilt line border. *The Victoria & Albert Museum.*

Plate 124
COFFEE CUP. D 2⅝in (66mm) Ht 2¾in (69mm).
Neale, marked P in gold inside the foot rim, sixteen flutes shanked from right to left alternating with acanthus leaves, plain loop handle, gilt line border. *Private Collection.*

Plate 125
TEA BOWL. D 3⅛in (79mm) Ht 2¹⁄₁₆in (52mm).
Derby, puce crown and baton mark, sixteen flutes shanked from right to left, alternating with acanthus leaves of almost even height (compare those on the Neale tea bowl in Plate 123), decorated in blue and gold. *Micawber Antiques, Wingham, Kent.*

Plate 126
COFFEE CUP. D 2¹¹⁄₁₆in (68mm) Ht 2⁹⁄₁₆in (64mm).
Factory unknown, no mark, poor quality greyish body with good greenish translucency, eighteen flutes shanked from right to left, decorated with small pink and green flowers. *The Berthoud Collection.*

Plate 127
COFFEE CUP. D 2⅜in (66mm) Ht 2⅜in (66mm).
Derby, puce crown and baton mark, tapered cup with sixteen vertical facets decorated with a blue line and gilt pattern, plain loop handle. *Micawber Antiques, Wingham, Kent.*

Plate 128
COFFEE CUP. D 2⁷⁄₁₆in (61mm) Ht 2⁷⁄₁₆in (61mm).
New Hall, no mark, hard paste cup with sixteen vertical facets, decorated with a simple gold border pattern, plain loop handle (see Holgate (3) Plate 24). *The Berthoud Collection.*

Plate 129
TEA CUP. D 3⅜in (86mm) Ht 2⅜in (60mm).
Coalport, no mark, Bute shape cup with eighteen vertical facets, decorated with a band of buff ground colour and gilding, plain loop handle. *Bill Dickenson, Ironbridge.*

Plate 130
COFFEE CAN. D 3¹¹⁄₁₆in (94mm) Ht 2½in (63mm).
Coalport, no mark, straight sided can with sixteen vertical facets in a greyish body, decorated with a black band and gilding, plain loop handle. *The Berthoud Collection.*

Plate 131
TEA CUP. D 3⁵⁄₁₆in (84mm) Ht 2⁵⁄₁₆in (58mm).
Minton, marked with the Minton 'Sèvres' mark and letter M in blue but with no pattern number, Bute shape with eighteen facets and loop handle and with a pink and gold border not corresponding to a Minton pattern, probably made by Minton's as a replacement to match a Coalport service. *The Berthoud Collection.*

Plate 132
TEA CUP. D 3in (76mm) Ht 2⁷⁄₁₆in (61mm).
Derby, puce crown and baton mark, Bute shape cup with eighteen vertical facets, decorated with a blue border, gilt band and pineapple gilding. *Private Collection.*

Plate 133
TEA CUP. D 3⅛in (79mm) Ht 2⅜in (60mm).
Miles Mason, no mark, Bute shape cup with twenty vertical facets, decorated with a pattern of three leafed flowers and gilding, ring handle with thumb rest pointing away from the cup. *Christopher May.*

Plate 134
COFFEE CAN. D 2¹¹⁄₁₆in (68mm) Ht 2⅝in (66mm).
Miles Mason, no mark, coffee can matching the cup shown in Plate 133, twenty vertical facets. decorated with orange flowers and gilding, typical thumb rest handle. *The Haggar Collection, City Museum & Art Gallery, Stoke-on-Trent.*

Plate 135
TEA CUP. D 3in (76mm) Ht 2⅜in (60mm).
Pinxton, no mark, Bute shape cup with eighteen vertical facets, decorated with blue harebells and gilding, loop handle following a very distinctive curve (compare Plate 141). *The Berthoud Collection.*

Plate 136
COFFEE CAN. D 2⅝in (66mm) Ht 2½in (63mm).
New Hall, no mark, hard paste can with sixteen vertical facets, decorated with a gilt rim, handle with circular ring typical of New Hall hard paste cups pressed against the body, no thumb rest. *Micawber Antiques, Wingham, Kent.*

Plate 137
COFFEE CUP. D 2⅜in (60mm) Ht 2⅜in (60mm).
Factory X, no mark (see Holgate (3)), cup with sixteen vertical flutes, decorated with a purple and gold pattern, plain loop handle. *Private Collection.*

Plate 138
COFFEE CUP. D 2¹⁵⁄₁₆in (74mm) Ht 2⁵⁄₁₆in (58mm).
Derby, blue crown mark, greyish pitted paste with sixteen vertical facets, decorated with enamelled flowers, plain loop handle. *Private Collection.*

Plate 139
COFFEE CUP. D 2¾in (69mm) Ht 2¹¹/₁₆in (68mm).
Factory unknown, no mark, barely translucent body, heavily crazed glaze, enamelled chinoiserie pattern, kicked handle similar to Factory Z (compare Plates 146-148). *Christopher May.*

Plate 140
COFFEE CUP. D 2½in (63mm) Ht 2½in (63mm).
New Hall, no mark, hard paste cup decorated with an orange flower pattern, plain loop handle. *City Museum and Art Gallery, Stoke-on-Trent.*

Plate 141
TEA CUP. D 3¼in (82mm) Ht 2¼in (56mm).
Pinxton, pattern number 282, Bute shape cup decorated with maroon and gilt pattern, the loop handle following a distinctive curve (compare Plate 135). *Jean Sewell Antiques.*

Plate 142
COFFEE CAN. D 2¹⁵/₁₆in (74mm) Ht 2⅜in (60mm).
Pinxton, pattern number 282, can matching the tea cup shown in Plate 141, decorated in maroon and gilt, the can handle follows a different line similar to the Chamberlain kicked handle (Plate 107). *Jean Sewell Antiques.*

Plate 143
TEA CUP. D 3⅛in (79mm) Ht 2⅝in (66mm).
Derby, red crown and baton mark, and pattern number 659, Bute shape cup with loop handle decorated with a dark blue and gold pattern, plain loop handle. *Gus Brain.*

Plate 144
COFFEE CAN. D 2⁹/₁₆in (64mm) Ht 2½in (63mm).
Derby, red crown and baton mark, Bute shape decorated with gilt grapes and blue leaves, plain loop handle. *The Berthoud Collection.*

Plate 145
COFFEE CAN. D 2⁹⁄₁₆in (64mm) Ht 2⅝in (66mm).
Sèvres, interlaced Ls in gold, hard paste can decorated with dark blue ground colour, raised gilding and 'jewels' of raised enamel, kicked loop handle. *The Royal Museum, Canterbury, Kent.*

Plate 146
TEA CUP. D 3⅜in (86mm) Ht 2¼in (56mm).
Coalport, no mark, Bute shape decorated with blue and gold and armorial shield, kicked loop handle. *Bill Dickenson, Ironbridge.*

Plate 147
TEA CUP. D 3⅜in (86mm) Ht 2¼in (56mm).
Factory Z, no mark but similar to pattern 151, decorated with a bat printed in black of a classical scene, black enamelled edge, typical kicked loop handle. *Philip Miller.*

Plate 148
COFFEE CUP. D 2⅝in (66mm) Ht 2½in (63mm).
Factory Z, marked No 38, coffee cup matching the tea cup shown in Plate 147, decorated with a grey patterned border inside and with a typical kicked loop handle. *Philip Miller.*

Plate 149
TEA CUP. D 3³⁄₁₆in (81mm) Ht 2¼in (56mm).
Derby, puce crown and baton mark, waisted body and slightly scalloped edge, a shape common to both the Meissen and Sèvres factories, decorated with gilt swags and an inner border. *Gus Brain.*

Plate 150
COFFEE CUP. D 2¹⁵⁄₁₆in (74mm) Ht 2⅞in (72mm).
Derby, puce baton mark, waisted pear shaped cup decorated with a barbeaux pattern and with dontil edge inside, plain loop handle. *The Berthoud Collection.*

Plate 151
CAUDLE CUP D 3¾in (95mm) Ht 2¾in (69mm).
Worcester, Chinese seal mark in blue, waisted cup with scalloped edge, decorated with a scale blue ground with enamelled flowers and stylised insects, single handle with snake finial. *J. Robinson, Stroud.*

Plate 152
CAUDLE CUP. D 4in (101mm) Ht 3¼in (82mm).
Caughley, painted S mark in blue, of similar shape to the Worcester cup shown in Plate 151, decorated with a blue painted Dresden spray. *Bill Dickenson, Ironbridge.*

Plate 153
CAUDLE CUP. D 3¾in (95mm) Ht 3in (76mm).
Derby, puce crown and baton mark, and pattern number 500, waisted cup with plain unmoulded upper body, snake finial less pronounced than at Worcester and Caughley, decorated with an orange ribbon and gilt pattern. *Private Collection.*

Plate 154
TEA CUP. D 3⁵⁄₁₆in (84mm) Ht 2½in (63mm).
Chamberlain, no mark, pattern number 75, waisted cup in a hard greyish body with very large kicked handle. Decorated with the 'Dragon in Compartment' pattern. *The Dyson Perrins Museum, Worcester.*

Plate 155
TEA CUP. D 3¼in (82mm) Ht 2⅜in (60mm).
Caughley, painted S mark in blue, 'Tournai shape' decorated with painted swags of blue flowers, the decoration and handle reminiscent of Bristol wares (compare Plates 85 and 163) *Bill Dickenson, Ironbridge.*

Plate 156
COFFEE CUP. D 2¾in (69mm) Ht 2⅝in (66mm).
Caughley, painted S mark, of similar shape and decoration to Plate 155 but without the inner spur to the handle. *Bill Dickenson, Ironbridge.*

Plate 157
TEA CUP. D 3⅜in (86mm) Ht 2¼in (56mm).
Chamberlain, no mark, of Bute shape with large kicked handle, decorated with orange and blue flowers with green leaves. *Philip Miller.*

Plate 158
TEA CUP.
Neale, mark impressed 'Neale & Co.', Bute shape bone china cup with kicked handle, decorated with a Wedgwood type pattern in green and gold (see Haggar & Mankowitz (20) Plate III (A)). *Photograph reproduced by courtesy of R.G. Haggar.*

Plate 159
TEA CUP. D 4¼in (107mm) Ht 2⅜in (60mm).
Caughley, the saucer marked S in blue, shallow cup decorated with flowers painted in blue and gilt border, rather small loop handle. *Bill Dickenson, Ironbridge.*

Plate 160
TEA CUP. D 3⅛in (79mm) Ht 2¼in (56mm).
Caughley, marked S in blue and 45 in gold, Bute shape cup decorated with painted blue flowers, well formed kick handle (see Godden (4) Plate 51). *Godden Collection, Clive House Museum, Shrewsbury.*

Plate 161
TEA CUP. D 3⅛in (79mm) Ht 2³⁄₁₆in (55mm).
New Hall, no mark, hard paste Bute shape cup decorated with a pink and gold border and painted landscape panel, rare form of handle (see Holgate (3) Plate 54). *Jean Sewell Antiques.*

Plate 162
COFFEE CUP. D 2½in (63mm) Ht 2½in (63mm).
New Hall, no mark, hard paste cup matching the tea cup shown in Plate 161 but with plain loop handle, the kick handle apparently not used on coffee cups. *Jean Sewell Antiques.*

Plate 163
TEA CUP. D 3in (76mm) Ht 2in (50mm).
Bristol hard paste cup, marked 3 c. 1770-1778, of waisted form copying Meissen, typical handle, decorated with swags of enamelled flowers. *Micawber Antiques, Wingham, Kent.*

Plate 164
CAUDLE CUP. D 3¹¹⁄₁₆in (68mm) Ht 2¾in (69mm).
Caughley, S mark in blue, waisted caudle cup decorated with the blue transfer printed 'Fitzhugh' border, deeply kicked handle. *Clive House Museum, Shrewsbury.*

Plate 165
TEA CUP. D 3⅛in (79mm) Ht 1¹⁵⁄₁₆in (49mm).
Chelsea-Derby, gilt anchor/D mark, moulded base cup decorated with green swags, blue and gold rim and base moulding, distinctive flat topped handle. *The Royal Museum, Canterbury, Kent.*

Plate 166
TEA CUP. D 3⅞in (98mm) Ht 2⅛in (53mm).
Derby, puce crown and baton mark and impressed F, fluted base cup decorated in blue and gold, flat topped handle. *Christopher May.*

Plate 167
TEA CUP. D 3¹⁄₁₆in (78mm) Ht 2½in (63mm).
Derby, puce crown and baton mark, Bute shape cup with plain loop handle, decorated with an orange ground colour and gilding. *Private Collection.*

Plate 168
TEA CUP. D 3⅛in (79mm) Ht 2⅛in (53mm).
Davenport, no mark, Bute shape cup of salmon pink stained earthenware lined with white slip and decorated externally with a black vine leaf pattern and black rim, plain loop handle (see Lockett (6) Plate 18). *Private Collection.*

Plate 169
COFFEE CUP. D 3⅜in (86mm) Ht 2⁵⁄₁₆in (58mm).
Derby, puce crown and baton mark, thinly potted cup decorated with a band of yellow and with a pattern of fawn 'bosses', plain loop handle. *The Berthoud Collection.*

Plate 170
COFFEE CUP. D 2⁹⁄₁₆in (64mm) Ht 2⅝in (66mm).
Derby, puce crown and baton mark, finely striated moulding wrythen from right to left, decorated with barbeaux swags, plain loop handle. *Private Collection.*

Plate 171
TEA CUP. D 3⅜in (86mm) Ht 2⅛in (53mm).
Neale, 'Neale & Co.' impressed, the saucer marked with a three-towered castle and 8 in red, Bute shape cup with plain loop handle decorated with a barbeaux pattern and gilding. *The Victoria and Albert Museum.*

Plate 172
COFFEE CUP. D 2½in (63mm) Ht 2⁹⁄₁₆in (64mm).
Neale, no mark, decorated with a band of enamelled flowers and gold rim, plain loop handle. *Private Collection.*

Plate 173
TEA CUP. D 3⅝in (92mm) Ht 2½in (63mm).
Coalport, no mark, of Bute shape with well formed loop handle in the form of a serpent, decorated with a pale blue ground, orange ovals with green centres. *Patricia Ratcliffe Antiques.*

Plate 174
COFFEE CAN. D 2¹⁵⁄₁₆in (74mm) Ht 2⅝in (66mm).
Coalport, no mark, greyish paste decorated with an Imari pattern, the loop handle in the form of a serpent. *Nigel Gasper Collection.*

Plate 175
TEA CUP. D 3⅜in (60mm) Ht 2⅝in (66mm).
Davenport, printed retailer's mark 'Sandbach and Co., King Street, Manchester' in a shield under a globe and 145, Bute shape cup with an Imari pattern in blue, orange and apricot. *D.R. Pomfret.*

Plate 176
COFFEE CAN. D 2½in (63mm) Ht 2½in (63mm).
Att. to New Hall, no mark, can with plain loop handle, decorated with an orange ground version of Spode's '878' pattern (see Whiter (7) page 179) in which the daisy flower has been formalised into a wheel. *City Museum & Art Gallery, Stoke-on-Trent.*

Plate 177
TEA CUP. D 3¼in (82mm) Ht 2⁵⁄₁₆in (58mm).
Wedgwood, brown printed mark, bone china Bute shape cup with loop handle, decorated with a yellow printed ground and enamelled chinoiserie pattern. *Private Collection.*

Plate 178
COFFEE CAN. D 2⅝in (66mm) Ht 2⅝in (66mm).
Wedgwood. brown printed mark, bone china can of excellent quality with plain loop handle, decorated with a continuous orange poppy pattern and gilt rim. *Private Collection.*

Plate 179
TEA CUP. D 3¼in (82mm) Ht 2¼in (56mm).
Wedgwood, WEDGWOOD impressed, earthenware cup decorated with an Imari pattern and with solid gilt loop handle. *Jean Sewell Antiques.*

Plate 180
COFFEE CAN. D 2½in (63mm) Ht 2⁹⁄₁₆in (64mm).
Wedgwood, WEDGWOOD impressed and printed O, earthenware can with plain loop handle decorated with an underglaze blue transfer printed floral pattern. *Private Collection.*

Plate 181
TEA CUP. D 3¼in (82mm) Ht 2⅜in (60mm).
Coalport, no mark, Bute shape cup of good quality with solid gilt plain loop handle, decorated with an Imari pattern in blue and orange. *The Berthoud Collection.*

Plate 182
TEA CUP. D 3⅛in (79mm) Ht 2⅜in (60mm).
Davenport, marked in puce 'Davenport, Longport, Staffordshire, Manufacturers to their Majesties', Bute shape with plain loop handle, richly decorated with a dark blue ground, panels of flowers and heavy gilding. *City Museum & Art Gallery, Stoke-on-Trent.*

Plate 183
TEA CUP. D 3⅝in (92mm) Ht 2³⁄₁₆in (55mm).
Davenport, from a service containing pieces marked 'Davenport, Longport', Bute shape with plain loop handle decorated with flowers formed of red spots and elaborate gilding. *Jean Sewell Antiques.*

Plate 184
COFFEE CUP. D 2¹³⁄₁₆in (71mm) Ht 2¹¹⁄₁₆in (68mm).
Davenport, pattern 26, porringer shaped cup with flared lip, corresponding to the tea cup shown in Plate 183, decorated with a feather pattern on a seeded ground similar to Minton's pattern 122 (see Plate 321). *Private Collection.*

Plate 185
TEA CUP. D 3⅜in (86mm) Ht 2½in (63mm).
Wedgwood, brown printed mark, thinly potted bone china Bute shape cup, decorated with a landscape by Cutts in purple monochrome. *Private Collection.*

Plate 186
TEA CUP. D 3⁵⁄₁₆in (84mm) Ht 2⁵⁄₁₆in (58mm).
New Hall, no mark, hard paste Bute shape cup with loop handle, decorated with a printed and enamelled Imari type pattern (see Holgate (3) Plate 138). *Jean Sewell Antiques.*

Plate 187
COFFEE CAN. D 2¾in (69mm) Ht 2½in (63mm).
New Hall, no mark, hard paste can of unusual shape with a well defined flared lip (seen to a lesser extent in New Hall cups and tea bowls Plates 28 and 82) apparently unique to New Hall, decorated with a printed and enamelled Imari pattern. *Private Collection.*

Plate 188
COFFEE CAN. D 2½in (63mm) Ht 2¾in (69mm).
Probably Turner, no mark, can with slightly concave sides and broad base, decorated with an Imari pattern in orange, blue and green enamels. *Private Collection.*

Plate 189
TEA CUP. D 3¼in (82mm) Ht 2¼in (56mm).
Miles Mason, impressed mark on the saucer, Bute shape cup decorated with purple vine leaves and red grapes, loop handle with characteristic thumb rest. *Jean Sewell Antiques.*

Plate 190
COFFEE CAN. D 2⁷⁄₁₆in (61mm) Ht 2¼in (56mm).
Miles Mason, no mark, bone china coffee can decorated with an orange, pale pink and gold lozenge pattern 284, loop handle with characteristic thumb rest (see Haggar and Adams (8) Plate 29). *The Berthoud Collection.*

Plate 191
COFFEE CAN. D 2⅜in (60mm) Ht 2⁷⁄₁₆in (61mm).
Davenport, stone china mark in blue, stone china can with eighteen scallops, loop handle with thumb rest, decorated with a blue transfer printed 'Chinese Bridge' pattern (compare Plate 175). *Private Collection.*

Plate 192
COFFEE CAN. D 2⁷⁄₁₆in (61mm) Ht 2⅜in (60mm).
Factory unknown, no mark, barely translucent ironstone type body, decorated with a painted chinoiserie pattern in blue, rudimentary thumb rest on the loop less well formed than on Miles Mason wares (compare Plate 190). *Private Collection.*

Plate 193
COFFEE CAN. D 2⅜in (60mm) Ht 2½in (63mm).
Factory unknown, no mark, unglazed cane ware coffee can with basket weave moulding to the base and moulded rim, decorated with a brown monogram and brown lines on the rim and loop handle. *Private Collection.*

Plate 194
COFFEE CAN. D 2⁷⁄₁₆in (61mm) Ht 2⁹⁄₁₆in (64mm).
Factory unknown, no mark, glazed earthenware can of a rich brown colour decorated with a gilt key pattern and with a large loop handle. *Private Collection.*

Plate 195
BREAKFAST CUP. D 3⅜in (86mm) Ht 2¹³⁄₁₆in (71mm).
Derby, red crown and baton mark, large cup with a distinctive pointed handle probably only to be found on Derby wares, decorated with a rural scene by Robertson. *Dover Museum.*

Plate 196
COFFEE CAN. D 2⅝in (66mm) Ht 2½in (63mm).
Derby, red crown and baton mark, can with distinctive pointed handle apparently peculiar to the Derby factory, decorated with a scroll pattern in purple, red, green, blue and gold. *M. Jacobs Antiques, Tenterden, Kent.*

Plate 197
COFFEE CUP. D 2⁹⁄₁₆in (64mm) Ht 2½in (63mm).
Derby, orange crown and baton mark and 9, can with unusual moulded handle, decorated rather crudely with enamelled flowers and with a gilt border inside and out. *Private Collection.*

Plate 198
COFFEE CAN. D 2¹³⁄₁₆in (71mm) Ht 2½in (63mm).
Factory unknown, no mark, slightly tapered can bearing a bat printed pattern signed Jas. Brindley. *The Victoria & Albert Museum.*

Plate 199
TEA CUP. D 3⅜in (86mm) Ht 2¼in (56mm).
Minton, Sèvres mark and pattern number 76, Bute shape cup of light weight body, loop handle with double kick (a similar form occurs on Ridgway and other wares), decorated with blue and gold forget-me-not sprays. *City Museum & Art Gallery, Stoke-on-Trent.*

Plate 200
COFFEE CAN. D 2⅝in (66mm) Ht 2⁵⁄₁₆in (58mm).
Minton, marked only K in sepia but corresponding to Minton's first series pattern 46 (see Introduction), the loop handle with double kick rises slightly higher than the rim and is slightly meaner than its Ridgway counterpart (see Plate 202). *The Berthoud Collection.*

Plate 201
TEA CUP. D 3¼in (82mm) Ht 2½in (63mm).
Ridgway, no mark, pattern number 445, Bute shape cup with double kick in the loop handle, decorated with light and dark blue ribbon and gilt 'fibres' with a gilt thistle inside. *Philip Miller.*

Plate 202
COFFEE CAN. D 2⅝in (66mm) Ht 2⅜in (60mm).
Ridgway, no mark, squat, thinly potted can with finely crazed glaze, generous loop handle with double kick, decorated with a band of apricot and gilding. *The Berthoud Collection.*

Plate 203
COFFEE CAN. D 3¾in (69mm) Ht 2¼in (56mm).
Coalport, no mark, squat can with double kicked handle, printed and overpainted with a picture of a fire engine. *Clive House Museum, Shrewsbury (lent by Tudor House Antiques, Ironbridge).*

Plate 204
COFFEE CAN. D 2¹⁵⁄₁₆in (74mm) Ht 2½in (63mm).
Davenport, brown wreath mark, decorated with a pattern similar to John Rose's pattern 696 (see Godden (9) Plate 73) and with a large loop handle similar to Coalport (compare Plate 203), probably made as a replacement for a Coalport service. *Private Collection.*

Plate 205
TEA CUP. D 3¼in (82mm) Ht 2⁵⁄₁₆in (58mm).
S & J Rathbone, marked SJR in a rectangular cartouche, plain edged Bute shape cup decorated with an underglaze blue printed 'Broseley' pattern, loop handle with double kick. *D.R. Pomfret.*

Plate 206
TEA CUP. D 3¼in (82mm) Ht 2⁵⁄₁₆in (58mm).
S & J Rathbone, marked R in a sunburst scalloped edged Bute shape cup decorated with an underglaze blue printed 'Broseley' pattern, loop handle with double kick. *D.R. Pomfret.*

Plate 207
TEA CUP. D 3⁷⁄₁₆in (61mm) Ht 2³⁄₁₆in (55mm).
Att. to Miles Mason, lozenge shaped seal mark in blue, Bute shape cup with slightly scalloped edge, decorated with an underglaze blue 'Willow' pattern, printed inner border. *Private Collection.*

Plate 208
COFFEE CAN. D 2⅝in (66mm) Ht 2⁵⁄₁₆in (58mm).
Att. to Ridgway, blue seal mark, squat coffee can with slightly scalloped rim decorated with an underglaze blue 'Broseley' pattern. *The Berthoud Collection.*

Plate 209
TEA CUP. D 3⅛in (53mm) Ht 2¼in (56mm).
Coalport, no mark, Bute shape cup in a greyish paste, decorated with a blue transfer printed 1798 'Pagoda' pattern, loop handle with single slight kick. *A.D. Willis Collection, Clive House Museum, Shrewsbury.*

Plate 210
COFFEE CAN. D 2½in (63mm) Ht 2½in (63mm).
Possibly Machin, no mark, bone china can of a highly translucent body of good quality, very light weight decorated with a bat print of a country house with trees, cows and a man on horseback. *The Berthoud Collection.*

Plate 211
TEA CUP. D 3⁵/₁₆in (84mm) Ht 2³/₁₆in (55mm).
Chamberlain, no mark, from a service in which the sucrier is marked 'Chamberlain's Worcester' in red, pattern number 424, Bute shape cup with inner spur on the loop handle with characteristic gold dots, decorated with red and gold buds. *Jean Sewell Antiques.*

Plate 212
TEA CUP. D 3⁵/₁₆in (84mm) Ht 2³/₁₆in (55mm).
Grainger, no mark, Bute shape cup decorated with a band of dark blue with a white quatrefoil pattern and gilding, rather heavily potted with inner spur. *Philip Miller.*

Plate 213
TEA CUP. D 3⁵/₁₆in (84mm) Ht 2¼in (56mm).
Miles Mason, no mark, Bute shape cup decorated with a band of enamelled flowers, loop handle following a flattened curve with small inner spur. *D.R. Pomfret.*

Plate 214
COFFEE CAN. D 2⁷/₁₆in (61mm) Ht 2⁵/₁₆in (58mm).
Derby, puce baton mark and 154, can decorated with two pale pink bands with gilding between, well rounded handle with pronounced inner spur. *Micawber Antiques, Wingham, Kent.*

Plate 215
COFFEE CAN. D 2⁹/₁₆in (64mm) Ht 2½in (63mm).
Pinxton, marked N5/A, can with band of barbeaux decoration and repeat pattern below, loop handle following a slightly oval curve with sharply formed inner spur. *City Museum & Art Gallery, Stoke-on-Trent.*

Plate 216
COFFEE CAN. D 2⁹/₁₆in (64mm) Ht 2½in (63mm).
Spode, pattern number 1194 in red, the upper part with a detailed panel of roses and multiple border, the remainder decorated in purple lustre to resemble marble containing fossil shells (pattern illustrated Whiter (7) Plate 217). *Private Collection.*

Plate 217
TEA CUP. D 3⁵⁄₁₆in (84mm) Ht 2⅜in (60mm).
Coalport, no mark, Porringer shaped cup with flared lip decorated with a gilt band and handle, the handle forming a tight loop with thick inner spur. *Bill Dickenson, Ironbridge.*

Plate 218
COFFEE CAN. D 2¹¹⁄₁₆in (68mm) Ht 2⅜in (60mm).
Coalport, no mark, can decorated with gilt rim only, the loop handle having a slight kick above the lower junction (compare Plate 209). *Bill Dickenson, Ironbridge.*

Plate 219
BREAKFAST CUP. D 4¹⁄₁₆in (103mm) Ht 3⅝in (92mm).
Factory unknown, no mark, probably made as a replacement for a Flight Barr and Barr Service, decorated with an apple green ground colour and gilt border, the large loop handle having a very pronounced inner spur and lower finial with gilt dots characteristic of a Worcester origin. *Jean Sewell Antiques.*

Plate 220
BREAKFAST CUP. D 3¹³⁄₁₆in (97mm) Ht 2⅝in (66mm).
Factory unknown, no mark, large coffee cup of Porringer shape matching the cup shown in Plate 219 and similarly decorated, the ornate handle formed as a scroll. *Jean Sewell Antiques.*

Plate 221
BREAKFAST CUP. D 4¼in (107mm) Ht 2¾in (69mm).
Swansea, marked SWANSEA in red enamel, Porringer shaped cup of duck egg paste c. 1816, the loop handle having an inner spur, factory decorated by William Pollard. *The Royal Institution of South Wales, Swansea.*

Plate 222
TEA CUP. D 3¼in (82mm) Ht 2in (50mm).
Davenport, unmarked, bone china Porringer shape with plain loop handle, decorated with a spray of roses. *Philip Miller.*

Plate 223
TEA CUP. D 3 5/16in (84mm) Ht 2¼in (56mm).
Spode, pattern number 1050 (c. 1806), Bute shape cup of fine white bone china decorated with a colourful Imari pattern, well formed kicked handle often referred to as a 'Spode type' handle. *The Berthoud Collection.*

Plate 224
COFFEE CAN. D 2 13/16in (71mm) Ht 2⅝in (66mm).
Spode, no mark but conforming to pattern 348, straight sided coffee can and decorated with a gilt chain pattern exceptionally well formed version of the kicked handle. *Christopher May*

Plate 225
TEA CUP. D 3 3/16in (81mm) Ht 2¼in (56mm).
Spode, marked SPODE in red and pattern number 1978, the popular 'Floral Embossed' shape (c. 1812) the moulded flowers reserved in white against a pale blue ground and with enamelled flowers inside. *R. Govier.*

Plate 226
COFFEE CAN. D 2⅝in (66mm) Ht 2½in (63mm).
Spode, marked SPODE in red and pattern number 1978, the tapered can matching the cup shown in Plate 225 in moulding and decorations. *R. Govier.*

Plate 227
TEA CUP. D 3 3/16in (81mm) Ht 2⅜in (60mm).
Spode, no mark, Bute shape cup with the rather rare 'Swag Embossed' moulding (the moulding illustrated Whiter (7) Plate 228), decorated with a gilt dontil border only. *The Berthoud Collection.*

Plate 228
COFFEE CAN. D 2 11/16in (68mm) Ht 2⅝in (66mm).
Spode, no mark, but conforming to pattern 1974, tapered can with the 'Swag Embossed' moulding (the moulding illustrated Whiter (7) Plate 228), decorated with small enamelled flower sprays and with the kicked handle rather poorly formed. *Miss Jones.*

Plate 229
TEA CUP. D 3¼in (82mm) Ht 2¼in (56mm).
Herculaneum, no mark, Bute shape cup decorated with a band of pale apricot, orange bars and gilt leaves, the kicked handle having a thumb rest set rather low down. *The Berthoud Collection.*

Plate 230
COFFEE CAN. D 2½in (63mm) Ht 2¹¹/₁₆in (68mm).
Herculaneum, no mark, straight sided can decorated with orange and gold and with a meander pattern of green leaves, finely crazed glaze, three spur marks below, thumb rest set low on the kicked handle. *Private Collection.*

Plate 231
TEA CUP. D 3½in (89mm) Ht 2⅜in (60mm).
Herculaneum, no mark, large Bute shape cup decorated with a pink bat print of sheep grazing, the kicked handle with almost rudimentary thumb rest. *Private Collection.*

Plate 232
COFFEE CAN. D 2⅜in (66mm) Ht 2¹¹/₁₆in (68mm).
Herculaneum, no mark, straight sided coffee can with slightly oily glaze decorated with a bat print of a country house and park, kicked handle with rudimentary thumb rest set low on the handle. *Gus Brain.*

Plate 233
TEA CUP. D 3⅜in (86mm) Ht 2¼in (56mm).
Herculaneum, no mark, large Bute shape cup decorated with a pale blue transfer printed 'Broseley' pattern, very slightly kicked handle with low thumb rest. *Jean Sewell Antiques.*

Plate 234
COFFEE CAN. D 2¹¹/₁₆in (68mm) Ht 2¾in (69mm).
Herculaneum, no mark, straight sided can matching the cup shown in Plate 233, decorated with a pale blue transfer printed 'Broseley' pattern, very slightly kicked handle with low thumb rest. *Jean Sewell Antiques.*

Plate 235
TEA CUP. D 3⁷⁄₁₆in (87mm) Ht 1⅞in (48mm).
Spode, printed mark SPODE in underglaze blue, 'Royal Flute' shape with slightly wavy edge decorated with a blue transfer printed 'Broseley' pattern, standard kicked handle (see Whiter (7) page 127). *The Berthoud Collection.*

Plate 236
COFFEE CUP. D 2½in (63mm) Ht 2⅝in (66mm).
Spode, printed mark SPODE in underglaze blue, 'Royal Flute' shape with slightly wavy edge matching the cup shown in Plate 235 (see Whiter (7) page 127). *The Berthoud Collection.*

Plate 237
COFFEE CAN. D 2½in (63mm) Ht 2½in (63mm).
Davenport, brown wreath mark, straight sided bone china can decorated with small enamelled flowers, loop handle with inner spur. *Private Collection.*

Plate 238
COFFEE CAN. D 2½in (63mm) Ht 2½in (63mm).
Davenport, blue wreath mark, very slightly tapered can decorated with a bat print of Stratford-on-Avon Church in black. *Private Collection.*

Plate 239
COFFEE CAN. D 2¾in (69mm) Ht 2⅜in (60mm).
Coalport, Anstice Horton and Rose factory, squat, slightly tapered can with wavy edge, decorated with a blue transfer printed 'Broseley' pattern, loop handle with pronounced inner spur. *G.A. Godden, Worthing.*

Plate 240
COFFEE CAN. D 2⅝in (66mm) Ht 2⅝in (66mm).
Miles Mason, blue seal mark, tapered can with flared lip decorated with a blue transfer printed 'Broseley' pattern, slender loop handle with flattened inner spur. *Private Collection.*

Plate 241
TEA CUP. D 2¾in (69mm) Ht 2⅝in (66mm).
Herculaneum, no mark, large Bute shape cup with characteristic oily glaze, decorated with a blue transfer printed pattern of a country house among trees, 'Spode type' kicked handle. *The Berthoud Collection.*

Plate 242
TEA CUP. D 3⁷⁄₁₆in (58mm) Ht 2⅜in (60mm).
Factory unknown, no mark, Bute shape cup from a service decorated with bat prints in black signed by Jas. Brindley (see Plate 198). *The Victoria and Albert Museum.*

Plate 243
COFFEE CAN. D 2⁷⁄₁₆in (61mm) Ht 2⁹⁄₁₆in (64mm).
Herculaneum, no mark, straight sided can with characteristic oily glaze, decorated with an Adam Buck bat print in black with a salmon pink border inside and black rim, heavily formed loop handle with double kick. *Private Collection.*

Plate 244
COFFEE CAN. D 2⅝in (66mm) Ht 2⅝in (66mm).
Att. to Miles Mason, blue seal mark, squat wavy edged can decorated with a blue transfer printed 'Broseley' pattern and with a blue border inside, loop handle with slight double kick. *Private Collection.*

Plate 245
COFFEE CAN. D 2½in (63mm) Ht 2½in (63mm).
Spode, pattern number 557, straight sided can decorated with a bat print in black of mountain scenery, tightly formed typical kicked handle (see Whiter (7) Plate 260. *Stocksprings Antiques.*

Plate 246
COFFEE CAN. D 2⅝in (66mm) Ht 2⁹⁄₁₆in (64mm).
Spode, pattern number 1922, straight sided can decorated with a bat print in black of children flying a kite, large and loosely formed kicked handle (see Whiter (7) Plate 259). *Christopher May.*

Plate 247
TEA CUP. D 3½in (63mm) Ht 2⁵⁄₁₆in (58mm).
W(xxx) factory, no mark, cup of French shape (so styled in early pattern books), decorated with a landscape in brown monochrome. These wares were previously attributed to Enoch Wood. *City Museum & Art Gallery, Stoke-on-Trent.*

Plate 248
COFFEE CUP. D 2⅞in (72mm) Ht 2¾in (69mm).
W(xxx) factory, no mark, coffee cup matching that shown in Plate 247, with slightly convex sides, greyish pitted body, decorated with landscapes in brown monochrome with gilt swags. *City Museum & Art Gallery, Stoke-on-Trent.*

Plate 249
TEA CUP. D 3¹⁄₁₆in (78mm) HT 2⅜in (60mm).
Coalport, no mark, Bute shaped cup with square handle, decorated with an Imari pattern in blue, orange and gold. *Jean Sewell Antiques.*

Plate 250
COFFEE CUP. D 2½in (63mm) Ht 2⁷⁄₁₆in (61mm).
Coalport, no mark, can in greyish hard body with square handle, decorated with two black bands, green leaves and gilding. *Private Collection.*

Plate 251
TEA CUP. D 3⅜in (86mm) Ht 2⁵⁄₁₆in (58mm).
Davenport, brown wreath mark, Bute shape cup decorated with enamelled flowers and gilding, square handle. *Private Collection.*

Plate 252
TEA CUP. D 3⁵⁄₁₆in (58mm) Ht 2³⁄₁₆in (55mm).
Coalport, no mark, French shape cup, decorated with an elaborate gilt pattern with an oval scenic panel, square handle. *Private Collection.*

Plate 253
TEA CUP. D 3½in (89mm) Ht 2,⁷⁄₁₆in (61mm).
Wedgwood, marked WEDGWOOD in red and pattern number 785, French shape with concave sides, decorated with a lily of the valley on a solid gilt ground. *Dr. Geoffrey & Alma Barnes Collection.*

Plate 254
COFFEE CUP. D 3⅞in (98mm) Ht 2¾in (69mm).
Wedgwood, marked WEDGWOOD in red, French shape cup decorated with a lily of the valley (pattern 785) on a solid gilt ground. *Private Collection.*

Plate 255
TEA CUP. D 3½in (89mm) Ht 2¼in (56mm).
Derby, red crown and baton mark and 726, Bloor Derby version of the French shape, decorated with dark blue leaves and gilding. The square handle grooved on either side. *Bill Dickenson, Ironbridge.*

Plate 256
TEA CUP. D 3⅜in (86mm) Ht 2⅜ (60mm).
Derby, red crown and baton mark and 745, intermediate shape between the French (Plate 255) and bucket (Plates 257 and 258) decorated with an orange ground colour and gilding. *Jean Sewell Antiques.*

Plate 257
TEA CUP. D 3⅝in (92mm) Ht 1¾in (44mm).
Derby, red crown and baton mark and 735, a heavy, squat bucket shaped cup decorated with gilding outside and with pink hearts and purple anthemion pattern inside, heavy square handle grooved on either side. *Jean Sewell Antiques.*

Plate 258
TEA CUP. D 3⅝in (92mm) Ht 1¹³⁄₁₆in (46mm).
Derby, red crown and baton mark, squat bucket shaped cup similar to that shown in Plate 257, the handle squarer and set at a lower level, decorated inside with red scrolls and green leaves. *The Berthoud Collection.*

Plate 259
TEA CUP. D 3¼in (82mm) Ht 1¹³⁄₁₆in (46mm).
Dresden, crossed sword mark in blue and the saucer marked Dresden 1739 in blue, hard paste cup with leaf moulded base and flared lip, decorated with an enamelled chinoiserie pattern, characteristic 'wishbone' type handle. *The Royal Museum, Canterbury, Kent.*

Plate 260
TEA CUP. D 3⁷⁄₁₆in (87mm) Ht 2³⁄₁₆in (55mm).
Derby, red crown and baton mark, porringer shaped cup with flared lip and Meissen wishbone handle, one of the most popular at the Derby factory, decorated with a typically colourful Imari pattern and with red and blue flowers within. *The Berthoud Collection.*

Plate 261
COFFEE CAN. D 2⁹⁄₁₆in (64mm) Ht 2½in (63mm).
Derby, red baton mark, straight sided can decorated with a broad band of pale pink and a pink, red and green pattern, Meissen wishbone handle. *The Berthoud Collection.*

Plate 262
COFFEE CAN. D 2⅝in (66mm) Ht 2½in (63mm).
Derby, red crown and baton mark, tapered can with scalloped edge, osier moulding and wishbone handle (both derived from Meissen) decorated with an armorial pattern from a service made for the 3rd Marquis of Hertford, KG. *The Victoria and Albert Museum.*

Plate 263
BREAKFAST CUP. D 4¹⁄₁₆in (103mm) Ht 2½in (63mm).
Derby, red crown and baton mark and 19, Bute shape of similar form to the can shown in Plate 262 but with plain loop handle, crudely decorated with large green enamel flowers. *Bill Dickenson, Ironbridge.*

Plate 264
COFFEE CUP. D 2¹³⁄₁₆in (71mm) Ht 2½in (63mm).
Factory unknown, no mark, cup with osier moulding and rare handle form, the upper attachment measuring ¾in across, decorated with enamelled flowers. *Private Collection.*

Plate 265
TEA CUP. D 3½in (89mm) Ht 2⅜in (60mm).
Miles Mason, no mark, Bute shape cup with very slightly translucent body, moulded osier border, blue and orange Imari pattern below, gilded two spur handle (see Godden (10) Plate 264). *Private Collection.*

Plate 266
COFFEE CAN. D 2½in (63mm) Ht 2½in (63mm).
Miles Mason, no mark, slightly tapered moulded can decorated with moulded flowers and with a complex handle. *Philip Miller.*

Plate 267
TEA CUP. D 3¼in (82mm) Ht 2½in (63mm).
Miles Mason, no mark, vine leaf moulded cup, the moulding reserved in white on a solid gilt ground (see Godden (10) Plates 99-101). The matching tea pot is in the form of a swan. *Mona & Gerald Sattin.*

Plate 268
COFFEE CAN. D 2⅝in (66mm) Ht 2½in (63mm).
Miles Mason, no mark, fine leaf moulded can, the moulding reserved in white against a pale blue ground, decorated with an enamelled bird's nest inside, the handle similar to that in Plate 267. *Philip Miller.*

Plate 269
BREAKFAST CUP. D 4⅛in (104mm) Ht 2³/₁₆in (55mm).
Miles Mason, no mark, Bute shape cup with sharply detailed floral moulding decorated with enamelled flowers inside and out, the handle of similar form to that in Plate 265 but more crudely modelled. *Private Collection.*

Plate 270
TEA CUP. D 3½in (89mm) Ht 2⅜in (60mm).
Miles Mason, no mark, Bute shape cup with floral moulding reserved in white against a blue ground decorated inside with enamelled flower sprays, the handle similar to that in Plate 265 but with additional feathering at the base (see Godden (10) Plate 100). *Philip Miller.*

Plate 271
TEA CUP. D 3⅝in (92mm) Ht 2¹/₁₆in (52mm).
Factory unknown, no mark, rather flattened Bute shape cup with rare handle form (see Haggar (20) Plate 79 where it is attributed to Spode), decorated with a variation of a New Hall pattern (see Halfpenny and Lockett (11) Plate 30) in red enamel and silver lustre, the handle set on lower than in the Minton version (see Plate 272). *The Victoria and Albert Museum.*

Plate 272
TEA CUP. D 3⁷/₁₆in (87mm) Ht 2³/₁₆in (55mm).
Minton, Sèvres mark and pattern number 252, Bute shape cup with rare handle form, the upper attachment close to the rim of the cup, decorated with a gilt ground and alternating birds and flowers in mauve and orange (compare Plate 271). *Philip Miller.*

Plate 273
COFFEE CAN. D 2¹⁵/₁₆in (74mm) Ht 2⁹/₁₆in (64mm).
Att. Adams, no mark, straight sided can decorated with a version of Spode's orange ground pattern 878 (499 at New Hall), the handle being rounder at the top than Minton's version (Plate 274), traditionally reputed to have been made by William Adams. *The Victoria and Albert Museum.*

Plate 274
COFFEE CAN. D 2⅜in (60mm) Ht 2⅜in (60mm).
Minton, marked 91 in puce, a poorly modelled can narrowing towards the rim, decorated with a fibre pattern in dark brown and six small flowers in brown, good clear body, handle more flattened and meaner than that in Plate 273. *G.A. Godden, Worthing.*

Plate 275
TEA CUP. D 3⁷/₁₆in (87mm) Ht 2¹/₁₆in (52mm).
Probably Minton, no mark, decorated with a version of Spode's 878 pattern (206 and 213 at Minton's), the handle set high on the cup as in Plate 272. *Gus Brain.*

Plate 276
COFFEE CAN. D 2¾in (69mm) Ht 2½in (63mm).
Factory unknown, no mark, bone china can with flared lip, decorated with a printed floral pattern enriched with enamel colours, unusual high loop handle. *Private Collection*

Plate 277
TEA CUP. D 3⅛in (79mm) Ht 2½in (63mm).
Worcester, open crescent mark, Bute shape cup decorated with
'Queen Charlotte's' pattern in blue and orange, pinched loop handle.
Northgate Antiques, Canterbury, Kent.

Plate 278
COFFEE CUP. D 2⅝in (66mm) Ht 2⅝in (66mm).
Worcester, no mark, straight sided cup with waisted base typical of
the Worcester factories, barbeaux decoration, pinched loop handle.
Dr. Geoffrey & Alma Barnes Collection.

Plate 279
TEA CUP. D 3¼in (82mm) Ht 2½in (63mm).
Chamberlain, no mark, Bute shape cup of hard greyish body, handle
characteristic of the Worcester factories, decorated with a yellow band
and a view painted in sepia of Windsor Castle. *The Dyson Perrins
Museum, Worcester.*

Plate 280
CUSTARD CUP. D 3⁵⁄₁₆in (84mm) Ht 2¹⁵⁄₁₆in (74mm).
Worcester, Flight Barr and Barr, no mark, pedestal cup with well
modelled handle, decorated with a typical blue berry pattern. *The
Berthoud Collectaon.*

Plate 281
TEA CUP. D 3¾in (95mm) Ht 2¼in (56mm).
Worcester, Flight Barr and Barr c. 1816, impressed crown and FBB
mark, cup of standard shape with gadrooned edge with typical
Worcester solid gilding, well modelled handle, decorated with large
brown leaves and small orange flowers. *The Berthoud Collection.*

Plate 282
COFFEE CUP. D 3⅜in (86mm) Ht 2¹³⁄₁₆in (77mm).
Worcester, Flight Barr and Barr, no marks, matching the cup shown
in Plate 281, decorated with a blue berry pattern and gilding. *The
Berthoud Collection.*

Plate 283
COFFEE CAN. D 2⅝in (66mm) Ht 2½in (63mm).
Chamberlain, from a tea service with the teapot market 'Chamberlain's Worcester' inside the lid, pattern number 274, tapered can in a greyish body with twenty double flutes shanked from left to right, with ring handle, decorated with a blue border and gilding. *The Berthoud Collection.*

Plate 284
BUCKET CAN. D 2⅞in (72mm) Ht 2½in (63mm).
Chamberlain, no mark, pattern number 274, tapered with slightly concave sides and scroll handle, companion to the porringer shape cup (Plate 289), decorated with a blue border and gilding. *Dover Street Antiques, Canterbury.*

Plate 285
TEA CUP. D 3½in (89mm) Ht 2½in (63mm).
Chamberlain, (from a service with marked teapot), Bute shape with very large ring handle, very white paste with pitted base, decorated with enamelled flowers inside and out. *Jean Sewell Antiques.*

Plate 286
COFFEE CAN. D 2¾in (69mm) Ht 2¹¹⁄₁₆in (68mm).
Chamberlain, no mark, pattern 276, tapered can in a greyish body with plain edge and large ring handle, decorated with a richly gilt Imari pattern. *The Berthoud Collection.*

Plate 287
TEA CUP. D 3⁵⁄₁₆in (84mm) Ht 2½in (63mm).
Grainger, no mark but from a service with painted mark 'Grainger Wood and Co. Worcester, Warranted, 232', faceted cup (known as 'Hamilton Flute' at Derby, see Plates 127-138), decorated with a gold and red leaf pattern, large, thickly potted ring handle typical of the Grainger factory. *The Dyson Perrins Museum, Worcester.*

Plate 288
COFFEE CAN. D 2⁹⁄₁₆in (64mm) Ht 2½in (63mm).
Grainger, marked 228 in gold, straight sided coffee can decorated with an orange ribbon and gilding, typical large thickly potted ring handle. *The Dyson Perrins Museum, Worcester.*

Plate 289
TEA CUP. D 3¹⁵⁄₁₆in (100mm) Ht 2⅜in (60mm).
Chamberlain, no mark, of porringer shape with scroll handle, a later development of the ring handle, decorated with the 'Stormont' pattern of seaweed gilding. *The Berthoud Collection.*

Plate 290
COFFEE CUP. D 3⅛in (79mm) Ht 2½in (63mm).
Spode, marked SPODE in grey, porringer shape cup with flared lip, decorated with enamelled roses, scroll handle of a type more commonly associated with the Chamberlain factory, probably Spode's 'Antique Shape' (see Whiter (7) page 131). *Private Collection.*

Plate 291
BUCKET CAN. D 2⅞in (72mm) Ht 2½in (63mm).
Chamberlain, marked in puce script 'Chamberlain's Worcester' and 'Heartsease'. Delicately modelled slightly concave sided can with scroll handle. Decorated with an enamelled Heartsease and gilt rim and with graded gilt dots round the handle characteristic of the Worcester factories. *The Berthoud Collection.*

Plate 292
BUCKET CAN. D 3¹⁵⁄₁₆in (100mm) Ht 2¾in (69mm).
Charles Bourne, marked CB/630, of a shape and border moulding similar to Chamberlain's but with the handle joined by the lower scroll only, decorated with single flowers and gilt sprays (compare also Plate 290).*Private Collection.*

Plate 293
BUCKET CAN. D 3¹⁄₁₆in (78mm) Ht 2⁹⁄₁₆in (64mm).
Chamberlain, marked 'Chamberlain's Worcester' in red script, gadrooned edge, blue ground with oak leaves and acorns reserved and decorated in brown, the ring handle developed with feathering and a 'fan' joining the upper and lower supports. *The Berthoud Collection.*

Plate 294
BUCKET CAN. D 3¹⁄₁₆in (78mm) Ht 2⅝in (66mm).
Chamberlain, no mark, pattern number 964, tapered with slightly concave sides and ring handle with eagle's head finial, decorated with a lilac ground with oeil-de-perdrix gilding and single flowers inside. *The Berthoud Collection.*

Plate 295
TEA CUP. D 3¼in (82mm) Ht 2¼in (56mm).
Miles Mason, no mark, bone china cup with flared lip, decorated with enamelled flowers, ring handle with thumb rest sloping away from the cup. *Christopher May.*

Plate 296
TEA CUP. D 3¹/₁₆in (78mm) Ht 2⅛in (53mm).
Davenport, blue seal mark, porringer shape with flared lip, decorated with an underglaze blue 'Broseley' print, ring handle with thumb rest in the form of a vertical spur. *Christopher May.*

Plate 297
TEA CUP. D 3⁵/₁₆in (84mm) Ht 2¼in (56mm).
Miles Mason, no mark, porringer shape decorated with an orange band and gilding between two borders of purple bell flowers, ring handle with thumb rest pointing horizontally away from the cup. *Haggar Collection, City Museum & Art Gallery, Stoke-on-Trent.*

Plate 298
TEA CUP. D 3⅛in (79mm) Ht 2¹/₁₆in (52mm).
Factory unknown, probably W(xxx), no mark, 'Worcester Shape' cup (compare Plates 303-305, 311 and 312), decorated with a landscape in orange monochrome, ring handle with small spur pointing slightly towards the cup. *Philip Miller.*

Plate 299
BREAKFAST CUP. D 4⁷/₁₆in (113mm) Ht 2⅝in (66mm).
Ridgway, marked 388, early Ridgway porringer shape decorated with a blue ground, blue flowers, seeded gilding and leaves, loop handle and double kick (compare Plates 199-204). *Christopher May.*

Plate 300
TEA CUP. D 3¼in (82mm) Ht 2½in (63mm).
Davenport, brown wreath mark and pattern number 1/G, decorated (possibly by Gould) with a buff ground and reserved panel with roses flanked by green leaves, ring handle with thumb rest. *Private Collection.*

Plate 301
TEA CUP. D 3⅛in (79mm) Ht 2½in (63mm).
Worcester, Barr period c. 1792-1807, incised B, slightly greyish paste, decorated with a blue and gold border, large thinly potted ring handle with typical Worcester 'tail'. *The Berthoud Collection.*

Plate 302
COFFEE CAN. D 2⁷⁄₁₆in (61mm) Ht 2⅜in (60mm).
Worcester, Barr period c. 1792-1807, incised B, straight sided can decorated with a bat print of shells in brown, typical generous ring handle. *The Berthoud Collection.*

Plate 303
TEA CUP. D 3¼in (82mm) Ht 2½in (63mm).
Worcester, Barr period, incised B, Bute shape with typical Worcester waisted base, decorated with a pattern of brown leaves and gilt lines, large ring handle. *The Berthoud Collection.*

Plate 304
COFFEE CUP. D 2¹¹⁄₁₆in (68mm) Ht 2⅝in (66mm).
Worcester, Barr period, incised B and 4 painted in brown, decorated with a pattern of brown grapes and vine leaves and slight gilding, the handle much thicker than in Plate 301-303. *The Berthoud Collection.*

Plate 305
TEA CUP. D 3³⁄₁₆in (81mm) Ht 2½in (63mm).
Worcester, Barr Flight and Barr period 1807-1813, impressed crown and BFB, decorated with a meander pattern of brown leaves and gilding, typical ring handle. *The Berthoud Collection.*

Plate 306
COFFEE CAN. D 2⅜in (60mm) Ht 2½in (63mm).
Worcester, Barr Flight and Barr period 1807-1813, impressed crown and BFB mark, decorated with a bat print of single flowers in black with typical ring handle. *The Berthoud Collection.*

Plate 307
TEA CUP. D 3⅜in (86mm) Ht 2½in (63mm).
Swansea, no mark, narrow based Bute shape cup with delicate ring handle with the lower finial turned away from the cup, decorated with flowers by William Billingsley. *The National Museum of Wales, Cardiff.*

Plate 308
COFFEE CAN. D 2³⁄₁₆in (71mm) Ht 2¾in (69mm).
Nantgarw, no mark, can with delicate ring handle, the finial turning away from the base of the can, decorated with enamelled flowers and scrolls of gilt leaves. *The National Museum of Wales, Cardiff.*

Plate 309
TEA CUP. D 3¼in (82mm) Ht 2¼in (56mm).
Davenport, pattern 310 in red, porringer shape bone china cup decorated with an enamelled bird in a tree pattern and gilding inside. *Private Collection.*

Plate 310
COFFEE CAN. D 2⁷⁄₁₆in (61mm) Ht 2⅜in (60mm).
Machin, pattern number 242, straight sided coffee can decorated with a dark blue ground colour with yellow drapes and gilding, thinly potted ring handle with no 'tail'. *Philip Miller.*

Plate 311
TEA CUP. D 3⅛in (79mm) Ht 2³⁄₁₆in (55mm).
Probably W(xxx), no mark, greyish hard paste cup, decorated with a blue and apricot pattern and gilding, ring handle with small vertical spur (compare Plate 298). *The Berthoud Collection.*

Plate 312
TEA CUP. D 2¾in (69mm) Ht 2¼in (56mm).
Probably W(xxx), no mark, 'Worcester' shape cup of smooth glassy body, decorated with a blue meander pattern, ring handle with small vertical spur. *City Museum & Art Gallery, Stoke-on-Trent.*

Plate 313
TEA CUP. D 3³⁄₁₆in (81mm) Ht 2⅜in (60mm).
Grainger, pattern number 228, Bute shape cup with large thickly potted ring handle, decorated with an orange ribbon and gilding. *The Dyson Perrins Museum, Worcester.*

Plate 314
COFFEE CAN. D 2½in (63mm) Ht 2½in (63mm).
Grainger, no mark, straight sided can decorated with orange spots and gilding typical thickly potted large ring handle. *Gus Brain.*

Plate 315
TEA CUP. D 3¼in (82mm) Ht 2¼in (56mm).
New Hall, no mark, Bute shape hard paste cup decorated with a bat print of a cottage scene, typical ring handle (circular on hard paste wares, compare Plates 327 and 328) pressed well into the body of the cup. *The Berthoud Collection.*

Plate 316
TEA CUP. D 3⅜in (86mm) Ht 2in (50mm).
Probably Grainger, no mark, cup of unusual shape but with a thickly potted large ring handle typical of the Grainger factory, decorated with a red, green and purple dot pattern. *Philip Miller.*

Plate 317
TEA CUP. D 3⁵⁄₁₆in (84mm) Ht 2⅜in (60mm).
Machin, no mark, decorated with a printed chinoiserie pattern also found on Machin's London shape cups (see Plate 395), thinly potted ring handle with long lower support. *Philip Miller.*

Plate 318
COFFEE CAN. D 2⁹⁄₁₆in (64mm) Ht 2⅜in (60mm).
Machin, no mark, straight sided bone china can, decorated with Chinese figures in coloured enamels, typical large ring handle with long lower support. *The Berthoud Collection.*

Plate 319
TEA CUP. D 3½in (89mm) Ht 2¼in (56mm).
Minton, marked pattern number 134 (first series), waisted cup with twenty four shanks rising from left to right and turning left at the top, the ring handle typical but the shanking rare, decorated with a gilt pattern. *Mercury Antiques.*

Plate 320
TEA CUP. D 3¼in (82mm) Ht 2¼in (56mm).
Minton, Sèvres mark and pattern number 539 (first series) Bute shape cup with small, slightly oval ring handle, decorated with Chinese figures in rich enamel colours. *The Berthoud Collection.*

Plate 321
COFFEE CAN. D 2½in (63mm) Ht 2½in (63mm).
Minton, marked 'No 122' only, squat can (the dimensions of Minton cans show considerable variation) with neatly potted round ring handle (compare Machin Plate 318, New Hall Plate 315 and Herculaneum Plates 323-324) decorated with the popular feather pattern. *The Berthoud Collection.*

Plate 322
COFFEE CAN. D 2⁹⁄₁₆in (64mm) Ht 2⅜in (60mm).
Probably New Hall, no mark, straight sided bone china can decorated with a blue, orange and silver lustre pattern, oval ring handle (see Plates 327 and 328). *Private Collection.*

Plate 323
COFFEE CAN. D 2⁷⁄₁₆in (61mm) Ht 2⁹⁄₁₆in (64mm).
Herculaneum, pattern number 2/869, straight sided can decorated with a gilt seaweed pattern and enamel pink roses between two gilt leaves, the ring handle in the form of a figure 9 (compare Minton Plate 321). *Bill Dickenson, Ironbridge.*

Plate 324
COFFEE CAN. D 2⁹⁄₁₆in (64mm) Ht 2½in (63mm).
Spode, marked SPODE in gold, decorated with a blue and gold pattern and probably made as a replacement for a Herculaneum service, the handle closely resembling that in Plate 323. *Private Collection.*

54

Plate 325
TEA CUP. D 3⅛in (79mm) Ht 2⅜in (60mm).
Derby, red baton mark and pattern number 544, Bute shape cup with slightly flared lip, decorated with a simple border of blue and gold, oval ring handle flattened against the cup. *The Berthoud Collection.*

Plate 326
COFFEE CAN. D 2½in (63mm) Ht 2⅜in (60mm).
Derby, red baton mark and pattern number 544, straight sided can decorated with a simple blue and gold border with an oval ring handle flattened against the can. *The Berthoud Collection.*

Plate 327
TEA CUP. D 3⁵⁄₁₆in (58mm) Ht 2⅜in (60mm).
New Hall, no mark, thinly potted bone china Bute shape cup decorated with a floral pattern in black, oval ring handle typical of New Hall bone china wares. *City Museum & Art Gallery, Stoke-on-Trent.*

Plate 328
COFFEE CAN. D 2¾in (69mm) Ht 2⅜in (60mm).
New Hall, the saucer marked New Hall in a double circle, slightly tapered can with flared rim, decorated with a printed and enamelled pattern of roses, typical oval ring handle on New Hall bone china wares. *The Berthoud Collection.*

Plate 329
TEA CUP. D 3⅛in (79mm) Ht 2³⁄₁₆in (55mm).
Wedgwood, marked WEDGWOOD in red and pattern number 607, Bute shape bone china cup decorated with a printed and enamelled pattern of Chinese flowers and a bird, oval ring handle similar to that used at New Hall (compare Plates 327 and 328). *Dr. Geoffrey & Alma Barnes Collection.*

Plate 330
TEA CUP. D 3⅛in (79mm) Ht 2³⁄₁₆in (55mm).
Wedgwood, marked WEDGWOOD in brown and V, Bute shape bone china cup with sharply narrowed base, decorated with a Japan pattern of brown printed and enamelled leaves, oval ring handle. *Jean Sewell Antiques.*

Plate 331
TEA CUP. D 3¾in (95mm) Ht 1¹¹⁄₁₆in (43mm).
Miles Mason, no mark, bone china cup of flattened shape with twenty eight vertical flutes, decorated inside and out with a blue printed pattern of birds and flowers. *Private Collection.*

Plate 332
TEA CUP. D 3⅜in (86mm) Ht 2¼in (56mm).
Miles Mason, blue seal mark, Bute shape cup with scallop edge, decorated inside and out with a blue printed pattern of a Chinese scene with figures. *Private Collection.*

Plate 333
COFFEE CAN. D 2¾in (69mm) Ht 2⁹⁄₁₆in (64mm).
Miles Mason, no mark, bone china tapered can with twenty four vertical flutes and scalloped edge, decorated with enamelled flowers. *Private Collection.*

Plate 334
COFFEE CUP. D 2⅝in (66mm) Ht 2¹¹⁄₁₆in (68mm).
Keeling, no mark, earthenware cup decorated with a blue printed 'Chinese Bridge' pattern and with a brown rim, square handle. *Michael Wakely.*

Plate 335
TEA CUP. D 3¹⁄₁₆in (78mm) Ht 2¼in (56mm).
Factory unknown, no mark, possibly Shorthose, earthenware porringer shape cup decorated with a blue printed Chinese scene with geese, handle of unusual bamboo design. *Private Collection.*

Plate 336
TEA CUP. D 3⅛in (79mm) Ht 2in (50mm).
Factory unknown, no mark, possibly Shorthose, earthenware tea cup with slightly flared rim decorated inside and out with a blue printed repeat shell pattern, the handle of unusual bamboo design. *Private Collection.*

Plate 337
TEA CUP. D 3½in (89mm) Ht 2¼in (56mm).
Derby, red baton mark, standard London shape with typical handle, decorated with pink and red flowers and gilding, this shape of tea cup is usually accompanied by a narrower coffee cup of similar shape or, more rarely, by a coffee can. *The Berthoud Collection.*

Plate 338
COFFEE CAN. D 2⅜in (66mm) Ht 2½in (63mm).
Derby, red baton mark, decorated with a gilt oval pattern and leaves, one of the few examples of the Grecian type handle being used on a coffee can (recorded on a Davenport can, Cushion (12) page 150, and on a Minton can, Plate 342 below). *The Berthoud Collection.*

Plate 339
TEA CUP. D 3⁹⁄₁₆in (90mm) Ht 2³⁄₁₆in (55mm).
Worcester, Flight Barr & Barr period, impressed crown and FBB mark, cup of basic London shape, typical FB and B handle with feathered moulding, decorated with flowers in purple monochrome. *Private Collection.*

Plate 340
COFFEE CAN. D 2¾in (69mm) Ht 2⅜in (60mm).
Worcester, Flight Barr & Barr period, impressed crown and FBB mark, straight sided can with feathered handle, the companion to the cup shown in Plate 339, decorated with an orange band and gilding. *Gus Brain.*

Plate 341
COFFEE CAN. D 2¾in (69mm) Ht 2⁷⁄₁₆in (61mm).
Coalport, no mark, unusual can with slightly flared lip and sharply narrowed base, decorated with a colourful Imari pattern in blue and orange, the handle copied from a silver shape. *Private Collection.*

Plate 342
COFFEE CAN. D 2¹¹⁄₁₆in (68mm) Ht 2,⁵⁄₁₆in (58mm).
Minton, Sèvres mark and pattern 723, bone china can of excellent quality narrowing slightly at the base (compare Plate 341) decorated with a pinkish brown bat printed shell pattern, thinly potted handle of Grecian shape rarely found on cans (see Plate 338). *The Berthoud Collection.*

Plate 343
TEA CUP. D 3⁷⁄₁₆in (87mm) Ht 2¼in (56mm).
Spode, marked SPODE in red and pattern number 2213, c 1815, typically well modelled bone china cup of London shape, decorated with a Japan pattern in blue, orange and gold, gracefully curved handle. *The Berthoud Collection.*

Plate 344
COFFEE CUP. D 3in (76mm) Ht 2⁹⁄₁₆in (64mm).
Swansea, marked SWANSEA in red enamel and pattern number 233, London shape cup with more easily recognizable type of Swansea handle, the upright very broad and forming a pronounced ogee curve, decorated in blue and orange with a Japanese style set pattern. *The Berthoud Collection.*

Plate 345
TEA CUP. D 3⅜in (86mm) Ht 2¼in (56mm).
Swansea, no mark, London shape cup with the more easily recognised handle, the broad upright forming a strong ogee curve, decorated with panels of enamelled flowers and birds and gilding on a dark blue ground. *The National Museum of Wales, Cardiff (E. Morton Nance Bequest).*

Plate 346
COFFEE CUP. D 3⅛in (79mm) Ht 2½in (63mm).
Factory unknown, the saucer marked pattern number 192, cup of unusual design with a pronounced horizontal ridge halfway down, heavily curved handle with feathered top elaborately decorated with a Japan floral pattern outside, blue ground with gilt dots and stars with yellow panels inside and elaborate gilding. *The Royal Museum, Canterbury, Kent.*

Plate 347
TEA CUP. D 3¾in (95mm) Ht 2⅜in (60mm).
Swansea, marked Swansea in red script and pattern number N219, London shape with the narrow upright forming a single curve, less easily recognisable as Swansea, factory decorated with underglaze blue and enamels in the Japanese taste. *The Royal Institution of South Wales, Swansea.*

Plate 348
TEA CUP. D 3½in (89mm) Ht 2¼in (56mm).
New Hall, no mark but conforming to pattern 1160, London shape cup decorated inside with white flowers on a blue ground, pale green leaves and gilding, rather weak handle ending in an almost vertical terminal. *Doremy Antiques.*

Plate 349
TEA CUP. D 3⁹⁄₁₆in (90mm) Ht 2¼in (56mm).
Spode, marked SPODE in red and pattern number 3803, c. 1824, London shape cup with floral embossed design reserved in white on a grey ground and decorated with gilding (compare Plate 270). *The Berthoud Collection.*

Plate 350
TEA CUP. D 3⅝in (92mm) Ht 2⅜in (60mm).
H. & R. Daniel, no mark, pattern number 3867, London shape with ribbon and wreath moulding, decorated with flowers and butterflies, an unmoulded version probably occurs but has yet to be identified. *The Berthoud Collection.*

Plate 351
TEA CUP. D 3⅜in (86mm) Ht 2⅛in (53mm).
Ridgway, pattern number 2/202, London shape with embossed floral moulding, decorated with a pale lilac ground, the moulding reserved in white with gilt sprays. *Philip Miller.*

Plate 352
COFFEE CUP. D 3¹⁄₁₆in (78mm) Ht 2½in (63mm).
Chamberlain, no mark, London shape cup with Union Wreath (rose, thistle and shamrock) moulding reserved in white on a grey ground and with enamelled handle with characteristic graded gilt dots. *Private Collection.*

Plate 353
TEA CUP. D 3¹¹⁄₁₆in (94mm) Ht 2⅜in (60mm).
C.J. Mason, no mark, slightly translucent ironstone London shape cup with flared lip and embossed floral moulding, decorated inside and out with random enamelled flowers, heavy ungraceful handle (compare Plate 270). *Private Collection.*

Plate 354
COFFEE CUP. D 3¹⁄₁₆in (78mm) Ht 2¹¹⁄₁₆in (68mm).
C.J. Mason, no mark, funnel shaped ironstone coffee cup matching the tea cup shown in Plate 353, with heavy ungraceful handle. *Philip Miller.*

Plate 355
TEA CUP. D 3⁹⁄₁₆in (90mm) HT 2½in (63mm).
Charles Bourne, marked CB/341 London shape cup with palm leaf and wreath moulding (common to a number of Staffordshire factories) picked out in gilding and decorated with enamelled flower sprays, the handles of Charles Bourne's London cups show a considerable variation and are a very unreliable guide to identification (compare Plates 356, 373, 374, 375 and 377). *Private Collection.*

Plate 356
TEA CUP. D 3⁷⁄₁₆in (87mm) Ht 2⅜in (60mm).
Factory unknown, no mark, London shape cup with much larger palm leaf and wreath moulding and with a deeply convex handle, decorated with pink enamelled flowers and blue spots. *Private Collection.*

Plate 357
TEA CUP. D 3½in (89mm) Ht 2¹⁄₁₆in (52mm).
Davenport, brown wreath mark, pattern 111, London shape with vertical terminal, palm leaf and wreath moulding, blue and green barbeaux decoration. *Micawber Antiques, Wingham.*

Plate 358
COFFEE CUP. D 2¹⁵⁄₁₆in (74mm) Ht 2⁷⁄₁₆in (61mm).
Spode, marked SPODE, in red and pattern number 3510 c. 1822, London shape cup with finely modelled palm leaf and wreath moulding decorated with gilding only, typical handle with tightly curved upper finial. *The Berthoud Collection.*

Plate 359
TEA CUP. D 3⁹⁄₁₆in (90mm) Ht 2¼in (56mm).
Factory unknown, pattern number 540 in gold, London shape cup with well modelled floral embossing and gilt roses between, rather heavily formed handle. *The Berthoud Collection.*

Plate 360
COFFEE CUP. D 2¹³⁄₁₆in (71mm) Ht 2⅜in (66mm).
Factory unknown, pattern number 925 in red, London shape cup with well moulded floral embossing, decorated with pink roses and brown leaves. *The Berthoud Collection.*

Plate 361
TEA CUP. D 3⁷/₁₆in (87mm) Ht 2in (50mm).
Minton, Sèvres mark and pattern number 917 (first series), London shape rather heavily potted handle (more delicate versions occur see Plates 342 and 362) and slightly convex sides, decorated with a purple flower pattern and gilt rim. *The Minton Factory Museum, Stoke-on-Trent.*

Plate 362
COFFEE CUP. D 2⅞in (72mm) Ht 2½in (63mm).
Minton, Sèvres mark and pattern number 754 (first series), London shape cup of fine quality, decorated inside with a rich Japan pattern in orange and green, delicately modelled solid gilt handle (compare Plate 361). *Private Collection.*

Plate 363
TEA CUP. D 3⅜in (86mm) Ht 2⁵/₁₆in (58mm).
Davenport, brown wreath mark and pattern number 554, London shape cup with vertical terminal, decorated with dark blue panels and gilt paterae (see Lockett (6) Plate 80). *Private Collection.*

Plate 364
TEA CUP. D 3¾in (95mm) Ht 2⅜in (60mm).
Coalport, the saucer bearing the Society of Arts Felspar backstamp, London shape cup with later 'weak' handle with short and sharply curved lower support, decorated with apricot ground, blue leaves and gilding. *Gus.Brain.*

Plate 365
TEA CUP. D 3½in (89mm) Ht 2⅛in (53mm).
Ridgway, no mark, pattern number 2/240 London shape with pronounced foot rim glazed over, decorated wih pink flowers and gold leaves. *The Berthoud Collection.*

Plate 366
TEA CUP. D 3½in (89mm) Ht 2¼in (56mm).
Davenport, brown wreath mark and pattern number 609, of typical London shape decorated with a dark blue border enamelled flowers and a gilt motif of five gold rings (also found on Minton and Coalport wares). *Jean Sewell Antiques.*

Plate 367
TEA CUP. D 3¾in (95mm) Ht 2⅛in (53mm).
Coalport, pattern number 128, large London shape cup with flared lip in a dull blue/grey paste, decorated with a Japan pattern in blue and orange. *The Berthoud Collection.*

Plate 368
TEA CUP. D 3¾in (95mm) Ht 2¼in (56mm).
Coalport, no mark, London shape cup with flared lip, decorated with pairs of roses with gilt leaves. *Jean Sewell Antiques.*

Plate 369
TEA CUP. D 3⅝in (92mm) Ht 2¼in (56mm).
Coalport, Anstice Horton and Rose pattern number 998, London shape cup with flared lip decorated with a red and gold repeat pattern inside and gold spots and red lines inside and out. *The Berthoud Collection.*

Plate 370
COFFEE CUP. D 2¹⁵⁄₁₆in (74mm) Ht 2⁷⁄₁₆in (61mm).
Coalport, Anstice Horton and Rose pattern number 998, coffee cup with flared lip matching the tea cup shown in Plate 369. *The Berthoud Collection.*

Plate 371
TEA CUP. D 3¹¹⁄₁₆in (94mm) Ht 2¼in (56mm).
Factory unknown, no mark, sharply flared cup decorated with a landscape and figures, well formed handle with sharply curved terminal. *Philip Miller.*

Plate 372
TEA CUP. D 3⅝in (92mm) Ht 2¼in (56mm).
Factory unknown, no mark, London shape cup with widely flared lip, decorated with an enamel Chinese scene and a crudely painted rose inside, thickly potted 'drawn up' handle. *Maureen Russell Antiques.*

Plate 373
TEA CUP. D 3½in (89mm) Ht 2⅛in (53mm).
Factory unknown, probably Charles Bourne, London shape cup of good quality decorated with a floral spray outside and a single flower within, handle with very long lower support. *The Berthoud Collection.*

Plate 374
COFFEE CUP. D 2¹⁵⁄₁₆in (74mm) Ht 2½in (63mm).
Charles Bourne, marked CB/269, London shape cup decorated inside with forget-me-nots and speedwell, another handle form with longer upper shank. *City Museum & Art Gallery, Stoke-on-Trent.*

Plate 375
TEA CUP. D 3⁹⁄₁₆in (90mm) Ht 2¼in (56mm).
Charles Bourne, marked CB/301, London shape cup decorated with a dark blue band inside with gilding and a floral spray at the bottom of the cup. This handle form has the upper shank shorter than the lower. *City Museum & Art Gallery, Stoke-on-Trent.*

Plate 376
COFFEE CUP. D 2¹⁵⁄₁₆in (74mm) Ht 2½in (63mm).
Factory unknown, no mark, London shape cup decorated with a colourful Japan pattern similar to Charles Bourne's pattern 233 (see Godden (13) Colour Plate 1). *The Berthoud Collection.*

Plate 377
TEA CUP. D 3⁹⁄₁₆in (90mm) Ht 2¼in (56mm).
Charles Bourne, marked CB/350, London shape cup decorated with Japan type flowers in blue and orange and a blue border inside, handle with long lower support. *City Museum & Art Gallery, Stoke-on-Trent.*

Plate 378
COFFEE CUP. D 3in (76mm) Ht 2⁹⁄₁₆in (64mm).
Att. Charles Bourne, no mark, from a service with tea cups marked CB/376 similarly decorated with a gilt pattern but with the handles having a less pronounced finial, the coffee cups (as above) unmarked, possibly Bourne or replacements. *The Berthoud Collection.*

Plate 379
TEA CUP. D 3⁷/₁₆in (87mm) Ht 2½in (63mm).
Peover, no mark, from a service from which a saucer dish with impressed mark PEOVER (Hanley c. 1818-1822) is now in the Victoria & Albert Museum, decorated with 'Retreating Peasant' pattern naively painted in dull matt green with a matt brown vase and pink roses, thickly formed rather sagging handle. *Mercury Antiques.*

Plate 380
TEA CUP. D 3⁹/₁₆in (90mm) Ht 2⅜in (60mm).
Peover, no mark, from a service containing marked pieces, scallop edged cup decorated with a blue border with gilt dashes and a band of enamelled roses, probably typical, slightly sagging, handle. *D.R. Pomfret.*

Plate 381
TEA CUP. D 3⅝in (92mm) Ht 2½in (63mm).
Herculaneum, pattern number 1415 in red, London shape cup of highly translucent body, decorated with green oak leaves and gold acorns, small handle terminal. *Dr. Geoffrey & Alma Barnes Collection.*

Plate 382
COFFEE CUP. D 3¼in (82mm) Ht 2⅜in (66mm).
Herculaneum, no mark, London shape cup decorated inside and out with enamelled birds and flowers, neatly potted handle (see Smith (14) Plate 140). *The Victoria & Albert Museum.*

Plate 383
TEA CUP. D 3¹¹/₁₆in (94mm) Ht 2⅜in (60mm).
Herculaneum, pattern number 266, London shape cup with dark blue border and gilding and gilt roses, thickly potted handle. *Philip Miller.*

Plate 384
TEA CUP. D 3⅝in (92mm) Ht 2³/₁₆in (55mm).
Herculaneum, no mark, conforming to pattern 266 (Plate 383) but with much larger, more positive, solid gilt handle. *G.A. Godden.*

Plate 385
TEA CUP. D 3½in (89mm) Ht 2⅜in (60mm).
Factory unknown, marked B in a sunburst, London shape cup decorated with a stencilled pattern in a thick, inky blue, the mark recorded by Godden but not attributed (see Godden (15) page 709). *Private Collection.*

Plate 386
TEA CUP. D 3⁷⁄₁₆in (87mm) Ht 2⅛in (53mm).
Factory unknown, marked D in a sunburst (not recorded in Godden (15)), bone china London shape cup of orange translucency with slightly flared lip, decorated with a green printed and enamelled pattern. *Private Collection.*

Plate 387
TEA CUP. D 3⅜in (86mm) Ht 2¼in (56mm).
Chamberlain, pattern number 534, straight sided London shape cup with parallel handle, decorated with a gilt wave pattern inside and characteristic dots on the handle. *The Dyson Perrins Museum, Worcester.*

Plate 388
COFFEE CUP. D 2⅞in (72mm) Ht 2½in (63mm).
Chamberlain, from a tea service with the teapot marked 'Chamberlain's Worcester, 53 Picadilly London' and pattern number 695, London shape cup with slightly convex sides decorated with red berries and a gilt meandering motif. *Jean Sewell Antiques.*

Plate 389
COFFEE CUP. D 2¾in (69mm) Ht 2⅝in (66mm).
Att. Chamberlain, no mark, London shape cup with large handle decorated with an Imari pattern, presented by Mrs. Whatmore-Jones from a service at Chastleton House Oxon. *The Dyson Perrins Museum, Worcester.*

Plate 390
COFFEE CUP. D 2¹⁵⁄₁₆in (74mm) Ht 2⅝in (66mm).
Coalport, no mark, London shape cup decorated with a blue ground and panels of flowers and birds attributed to Thomas Martin Randall. *Bill Dickenson, Ironbridge.*

Plate 391
TEA CUP. D 3⁹/₁₆in (90mm) Ht 2¼in (56mm).
Hilditch & Son, marked H&S in a wreath, London shape cup of no great quality with flared lip, decorated with a printed Chinese scene with a pig, decorated with green enamels. *Bill Dickenson, Ironbridge.*

Plate 392
TEA CUP. D 3⁹/₁₆in (90mm) Ht 2⅜in (60mm).
Hilditch & Son, marked B&S in a wreath, straight sided London shape cup decorated with the same print as in Plate 391 but decorated in blue enamels. (Helm (21) Shape C1). *Bill Dickenson, Ironbridge.*

Plate 393
TEA CUP. D 3½in (89mm) Ht 2⅜in (60mm).
Hilditch & Son, marked H&S in a crowned wreath, London shape cup with printed Chinese scene pattern decorated in coloured enamels with white flowers reserved (the green parasol is common on Hilditch wares but is not exclusive to that factory). *The Berthoud Collection.*

Plate 394
TEA CUP. D 3⅜in (60mm) Ht 2⁵/₁₆in (58mm).
Mayer & Newbold, marked M&N/307, London shape cup decorated inside with enamelled 'House on a Hill' pattern, strongly curved handle. *Philip Miller.*

Plate 395
TEA CUP. D 3⁹/₁₆in (90mm) Ht 2¼in (56mm).
Machin, no mark, London shape cup decorated with an enamelled pattern of Chinese figures, brown rim and a floral border inside, very large high handle. *Philip Miller.*

Plate 396
TEA CUP. D 3⅝in (92mm) Ht 2⅜in (60mm).
Factory unknown, pattern number 348, London shape cup with flared lip, decorated inside with a dark blue ground, reserved panels and gilding, thick handle with short stubby terminal. *The Berthoud Collection.*

Plate 397
TEA CUP. D 3½in (89mm) Ht 2¼in (56mm).
Factory unknown, no mark, possibly Herculaneum, London shape cup of greenish, almost 'duck egg paste' translucency with an oily glaze, decorated with a meandering vine leaf and pink blossom pattern inside. *The Berthoud Collection.*

Plate 398
COFFEE CUP. D 2⅝in (66mm) Ht 2⁷⁄₁₆in (58mm).
Factory unknown, pattern number 2033 in gold, London shape cup of excellent quality, decorated with orange flowers and gilding, well formed handle. *The Berthoud Collection.*

Plate 399
TEA CUP. D 3½in (89mm) Ht 2⅛in (53mm).
Factory unknown, no mark, London shape cup with basket weave moulding, possibly copying New Hall (see Plates 483 and 484), decorated with crudely painted flower sprays. *Dover Street Antiques, Canterbury.*

Plate 400
COFFEE CUP. D 3¹⁄₁₆in (78mm) Ht 3⁹⁄₁₆in (90mm).
Factory unknown, no mark, London shape cup of fine quality decorated inside with underglaze blue with buff bordered cartouches, buff panels hatched with gilding and enamelled flower sprays, well modelled handle. *The Berthoud Collection.*

Plate 401
TEA CUP. D 3⁷⁄₁₆in (87mm) Ht 2½in (63mm).
Factory unknown, marked pattern number 578x, possibly Machin, decorated with enamelled flowers, curved handle. *Lionel Bellamy*

Plate 402
COFFEE CUP. D 2¾in (69mm) Ht 2⅜in (60mm).
Factory unknown, no mark, probably Chamberlain, London shape cup decorated with orange flowers and reserved white leaves on a lilac ground, dark blue and gold border. *The Berthoud Collection.*

Plate 403
COFFEE CUP. D 2⅜in (66mm) Ht 2⅜in (60mm).
Grainger, marked 'Grainger Lee, Worcester' in underglaze blue, London shape scallop edged cup decorated with an underglaze blue 'Broseley' pattern narrow handle with vertical terminal. *Robin Hildyard.*

Plate 404
COFFEE CUP. D 2¾in (69mm) Ht 2⁷⁄₁₆in (61mm).
Davenport, brown wreath mark, pattern 111, London shape with palm leaf and wreath moulding, blue and green barbeaux decoration and handle with vertical terminal. *Micawber Antiques, Wingham.*

Plate 405
TEA CUP. D 3⁷⁄₁₆in (61mm) Ht 2⅜in (60mm).
Factory unknown, pattern number 205 in grey, London shape cup with slightly convex sides and nondescript handle, decorated with a thickly painted pink rose with sepia leaves and pink and green bell flowers. *Maureen Russell Antiques.*

Plate 406
COFFEE CUP. D 2¾in (69mm) Ht 2¼in (56mm).
Factory unknown, no mark, London shape cup decorated with a blue acorn pattern with red dots and gilding. *Robin Hildyard.*

Plate 407
TEA CUP. D 3½in (89mm) Ht 2¼in (56mm).
Factory unknown, pattern number 719 in red, London shape cup with embossed Union Wreath (rose, thistle and shamrock) decorated with enamel colours, handle with tightly coiled terminal. *Dover Street Antiques, Canterbury.*

Plate 408
COFFEE CUP. D 2¹⁵⁄₁₆in (74mm) Ht 2¹⁵⁄₁₆in (74mm).
Factory unknown, no mark, possibly New Hall, decorated with a seeded gilt leaf pattern, unusual handle with terminal curled into a scroll. *Private Collection.*

Plate 409
TEA CUP. D 3½in (89mm) Ht 2⅜in (60mm).
Rathbone, printed mark R in a sunburst (formerly attributed to Ratcliffe) scallop edged London shape cup decorated with a transfer printed 'Broseley' pattern thinly formed handle with vertical terminals. *Robin Hildyard.*

Plate 410
COFFEE CUP. D 3½in (89mm) Ht 2⅜in (60mm).
Rathbone, printed mark R in a sunburst, from a service partly marked thus and partly 'SJR', scallop edged London shape cup decorated with a transfer printed 'Broseley' pattern, thickly formed handle. *Philip Miller.*

Plate 411
TEA CUP. D 3⁷⁄₁₆in (87mm) Ht 2⅛in (63mm).
Hilditch & Co., printed B & Co. in a rectangular cartouche, scallop edged London shape cup decorated with a transfer printed 'Broseley' pattern. *Christopher May.*

Plate 412
COFFEE CUP. D 2¹⁵⁄₁₆in (74mm) Ht 2½in (63mm).
Davenport, blue seal mark and pattern number 602, of typical London shape with characteristic handle, blue printed pattern. *Private Collection.*

Plate 413
TEA CUP. D 3⁹⁄₁₆in (90mm) Ht 2¼in (56mm).
Grainger, pattern number 1276, London shape cup with flared lip, decorated with a blue printed pattern and pink enamelled flowers, heavily modelled handle. *Philip Miller.*

Plate 414
COFFEE CUP. D 2¹⁵⁄₁₆in (74mm) Ht 2⅜in (66mm).
Grainger, pattern 1276, narrow coffee cup matching the tea cup shown in Plate 413, similarly decorated. *The Berthoud Collection.*

Plate 415
TEA CUP. D 3in (76mm) Ht 2in (50mm).
Swansea, no mark, flattened Bute shape cup with plain loop handle, decorated in London with panels of enamelled flowers on a pale blue oeil-de-perdrix ground inspired by Sèvres (a rare version, with Dresden handle, may be found, see John (23) Plate 26B). *The National Museum of Wales, Cardiff.*

Plate 416
TEA CUP. D 3in (76mm) Ht 2in (50mm).
Nantgarw, no mark, the cup of flattened Bute shape with a plain loop handle, the saucer with flat, unglazed base, London decorated with swags of enamelled flowers. *The Victoria & Albert Museum.*

Plate 417
TEA CUP. D 3½in (89mm) Ht 2in (50mm).
Factory unknown, no mark, shallow cup of very translucent body, decorated with pairs of roses and gilt leaves, solid gilt loop handle. *The Berthoud Collection.*

Plate 418
TEA CUP. D 3⁷⁄₁₆in (87mm) Ht 1⅞in (48mm).
Derby, red baton mark and 21, shallow cup decorated with roses and nightshade in purple monochrome, well formed loop handle. *The Berthoud Collection.*

Plate419
TEA CUP. D 3½in (89mm) Ht 1⅞in (48mm).
Copeland and Garrett, felspar back stamp in green, a shallow Bute shape cup with plain loop handle, probably made as a replacement for an earlier service decorated with an armorial device in Chinese export style and the motto 'Vincit Veritas' (see Whiter (7) Plate 161). *The Berthoud Collection.*

Plate 420
TEA CUP. D 3⁹⁄₁₆in (90mm) Ht 2in (50mm).
Moore, (Longton c. 1868-1875) impressed mark MOORE on the saucer, shallow cup with fawn ground and enamelled peony pattern in blue, pink and orange, loop handle. *Bill Dickenson, Ironbridge.*

Plate 421
TEA CUP. D 3¾in (95mm) Ht 2in (50mm).
Swansea, marked SWANSEA in red enamel, shallow Bute shape cup with kicked loop handle, decorated with a landscape in sepia monochrome. *The National Museum of Wales, Cardiff.*

Plate 422
TEA CUP. D 3⅛in (79mm) Ht 2³⁄₁₆in (55mm).
Swansea, no mark, small Bute shape with kicked loop handle, decorated with enamelled flowers. *The Berthoud Collection.*

Plate 423
TEA CUP. D 3⅞in (98mm) Ht 2¹⁄₁₆in (52mm).
Swansea, no mark, porringer shape cup with embossed floral design and kicked loop handle, gilt lines round the rim, base and handle. *The National Museum of Wales, Cardiff.*

Plate 424
TEA CUP. D 3⁷⁄₁₆in (87mm) Ht 2in (50mm).
Swansea, marked SWANSEA in red script, porringer shape cup of duck egg china c. 1816, with osier moulding after Meissen and with loop handle with pronounced kick, decorated with sepia flower sprays, perhaps by, or from a design of, William Billingsley. *The Royal Institution of South Wales, Swansea.*

Plate 425
TEA CUP. D 3⁷⁄₁₆in (87mm) Ht 2in (50mm).
Swansea, no mark, porringer shape cup with osier pattern moulding after Meissen, of duck egg china c. 1816, decorated (probably at the factory) with enamelled flowers. *The Royal Institution of South Wales, Swansea.*

Plate 426
COFFEE CUP. D 3¹⁄₁₆in (78mm) Ht 2⁵⁄₁₆in (58mm).
Swansea, the saucer marked Swansea in red script, straight sided cup with osier moulding after Meissen, of duck egg china c. 1816, loop handle with slight kick, factory decorated with a little gilding. *The Royal Institution of South Wales, Swansea.*

Plate 427
TEA CUP. D 3¼in (82mm) Ht 2¼in (56mm).
Chamberlain, pattern number 274, porringer shape cup decorated with a blue border, scroll handle. *Dover Street Antiques, Canterbury.*

Plate 428
BREAKFAST CUP. D 4⁷/₁₆in (113mm) Ht 3¼in (82mm).
Swansea, no mark, cup of porringer shape with plain loop handle, rather crudely decorated with a green ground enamelled flowers and brown rim. *The National Museum of Wales, Cardiff, E. Morton Nance Bequest.*

Plate 429
TEA CUP. D 3¾in (95mm) Ht 2½in (63mm).
Chamberlain, marked with a grey back stamp 'Chamberlain's Worcester, 155 New Bond Street, London', decorated inside only with a garter and the words 'Com Wigorn 1837', from the 'Judges' Lodgings Service', loop handle with inner spur. *The Dyson Perrins Museum, Worcester.*

Plate 430
COFFEE CUP. D 3⅜in (86mm) Ht 2¹⁵/₁₆in (74mm).
Rockingham, the saucer marked with a red griffin and pattern number 457 (c. 1826-1832), French 'Empire' shape cup with well modelled horse's tail and hoof handle. *Bruce Newmane.*

Plate 431
TEA CUP. D 3⅞in (98mm) Ht 2½in (63mm).
Rockingham, pattern number 725, French 'Empire' cup decorated with a blue transfer printed floral pattern enriched with gilding, horse's tail and hoof handle. *Bruce Newmane.*

Plate 432
CRINOLINE POT. D 4¼in (107mm) Ht 3¼in (82mm).
Rockingham, no mark, earthenware pot with flattened rim, decorated with a blue transfer printed 'Boys Fishing' pattern, plain loop handle. *Bruce Newmane.*

Plate 433
CABARET CUP. D 3³/₁₆in (81mm) Ht 3in (76mm).
Swansea, no mark, from an ornately modelled cabaret set decorated in London for Mortlock's of Oxford Street (the main dealers in Swansea porcelain) and probably ordered for Thomas Coutts, private banker to George III, at the time of the dispersal in 1922 this service numbered 249 pieces. *The National Museum of Wales, Cardiff.*

Plate 434
CABINET CUP. D 2¹¹/₁₆in (68mm) Ht 2⅜in (60mm).
Nantgarw, no mark, tall cup with loop handle terminating in a griffin's head the hinged brass mould for this handle was excavated on the Nantgarw factory site in 1935, London decorated with enamelled flowers. *The Royal Institution of South Wales, Swansea.*

Plate 435
CABINET CUP. D 3⅛in (79mm) Ht 3in (76mm).
Worcester, Flight Barr & Barr period c. 1813-1840, marked in script 'Flight Barr & Barr, Worcester, Manufacturers to their Majesties and the Royal Family', with moulded beads, eagle and serpent handle, three lion's paw feet, decorated with enamelled birds in gilt trees. *Mona & Gerald Sattin.*

Plate 436
CABINET CUP. D 2¾in (69mm) Ht 2¹⁵/₁₆in (74mm).
Davenport, brown wreath mark, pedestal cup with double handle ending in a mask, decorated with enamelled flowers and gilding. *Private Collection.*

Plate 437
CABINET CUP. D 2⁹/₁₆in (64mm) Ht 3in (76mm).
Davenport, pattern number 675x, decorated with white roses and green leaves on a gold ground, high loop handle. *Private Collection.*

Plate 438
COFFEE CUP. D 2⅞in (72mm) Ht 2¾in (69mm).
Davenport, marked DAVENPORT in underglaze blue and with the registered mark for 1854 and pattern number 2789, with moulded panels decorated all round with a continuous landscape in coloured enamels. *Private Collection.*

Plate 439
TEA CUP. D 3⅞in (98mm) Ht 1¾in (44mm).
Sèvres, printed circular mark in blue (c. 1835), Paris flute moulding and gilt striated handle, an earlier version of this cup provided the inspiration for 'Paris flute' cups made at Swansea, decorated with a slate blue ground and gilding. *Dr. Geoffrey & Alma Barnes Collection.*

Plate 440
TEA CUP. D 3¾in (95mm) Ht 1⅜in (35mm).
Swansea, no mark, shallow cup of duck egg china c. 1816, Paris flute moulding and striated high loop handle joining the cup at the top of the lip, factory decorated with enamelled flowers and gilding. *The Royal Institution of South Wales, Swansea.*

Plate 441
TEA CUP. D 3⅜in (92mm) Ht 2⅛in (53mm).
Swansea, marked SWANSEA in red enamel, shallow Bute shape cup with Paris flute moulding and high loop handle, china clay body c. 1816, factory decorated with enamelled roses and with gilt rim and solid gilt handle. *The Royal Institution of South Wales, Swansea.*

Plate 442
TEA CUP. D 3¾in (95mm) Ht 1¾in (44mm).
Swansea, no mark, shallow cup with Paris flute and high loop handle, decorated with an inner border of gilt shells, a bear's head in the centre and solid gilt handle. *The National Museum of Wales, Cardiff.*

Plate 443
TEA CUP. D 3⅜in (86mm) Ht 2³⁄₁₆in (55mm).
Factory unknown, no mark, bone china cup of good quality, honeycomb and floral moulding below a flared lip, high loop handle ribbed at the base. *The Berthoud Collection.*

Plate 444
COFFEE CUP. D 3¹³⁄₁₆in (97mm) Ht 2⅝in (66mm).
Factory unknown, pattern number 669 in red, coffee cup matching the tea cup shown in Plate 447, decorated with a simple blue border and gilding. *Jean Sewell Antiques.*

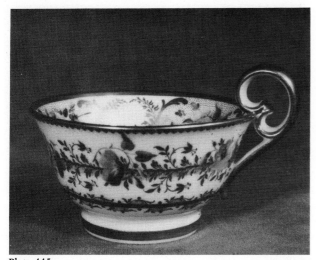

Plate 445
TEA CUP. D 3⅞in (98mm) Ht 2¹/₁₆in (52mm).
Nantgarw, no mark, cup with flared rim and kidney handle, the upper lobe noticeably larger than the lower. A rare form of this cup has a row of fine beads below the rim and round the well of the saucer which has a flat, unglazed base. London decorated with enamelled flowers and delicate gilding, and iridescent 'halo' round the flowers indicating London decoration. *The Berthoud Collection.*

Plate 446
COFFEE CUP. D 2⅞in (72mm) Ht 2½in (63mm).
Nantgarw, no mark, the cup with a flared rim and kidney handle, the upper lobe noticeably larger than the lower. London decorated with bands of enamelled flowers in an oeil-de-perdrix turquoise ground (see W.D. John (19) Plate 11a and page 105). *The Royal Institution of South Wales, Swansea.*

Plate 447
TEA CUP. D 4in (101mm) Ht 2³/₁₆in (55mm).
Coalport, pattern number 2/328, slightly scalloped flared rim with inner moulding, Nantgarw type kidney handle divided into two approximately equal lobes, decorated with enamelled flowers and hatched gilding. *Private Collection*

Plate 448
COFFEE CUP. D 3¹/₁₆in (78mm) Ht 2⅜in (60mm).
Coalport, pattern number 2/328, coffee cup matching the tea cup illustrated in Plate 447. *Private Collection.*

Plate 449
TEA CUP. D 3¹³/₁₆in (97mm) Ht 2⅛in (53mm).
Derby, Bloor Derby crown in a circle mark, cup with flared lip decorated inside with purple and pink scrolls and gilding, kidney handle with two roughly equal lobes. *The Berthoud Collection.*

Plate 450
COFFEE CAN. D 2⅝in (66mm) Ht 2½in (63mm).
Derby, orange crown and baton mark, straight sided can decorated with enamelled flowers and with a gilt dontil border inside and out, the use of a kidney handle on a can probably confined to Derby. *Private Collection.*

Plate 451
TEA CUP. D 3¹⁵/₁₆in (100mm) Ht 2in (50mm).
Coalport, pattern number 2/336, slightly scalloped moulded edge cup, decorated with a band of blue and delicate gilding, complex handle. *The Berthoud Collection.*

Plate 452
TEA CUP. D 3¾in (95mm) Ht 2³/₁₆in (55mm).
Coalport, the saucer bearing the Society of Arts Felspar back stamp and pattern number 848, the cup with flared unmoulded rim and Nantgarw type kidney handle divided into two approximately equal lobes. This type of handle was also used at Derby (Plates 449 and 450). Decorated in Paris style with elaborate gilding. *Jean Sewell Antiques.*

Plate 453
TEA CUP. D 3¾in (95mm) Ht 2¼in (56mm).
Ridgway, pattern number 2/3773, heavily potted cup with moulded rim on a pedestal foot, decorated with an apricot ground colour and deep orange leaves and gilding. Distinctive moulded ring handle. *Gus Brain Antiques.*

Plate 454
COFFEE CUP. D 3½in (89mm) Ht 3in (76mm).
Ridgway, pattern number 2/3773, heavily potted cup matching the tea cup shown in Plate 453. *Gus Brain Antiques.*

Plate 455
TEA CUP. D 3¹¹/₁₆in (94mm) Ht 2¼in (56mm).
Factory A (see Introduction), no mark, fluted cup shanked to the right with a flared lip, decorated with a dark blue ground, thin stemmed enamelled flowers and gilt anthemion and hatching, handle of distinctive type. *Private Collection.*

Plate 456
COFFEE CUP. D 3³/₁₆in (81mm) Ht 3¹¹/₁₆in (94mm).
Factory A, no mark but conforming to pattern 2287 on a matching sucrier, decorated with a dark blue ground, enamelled flowers and gilt spiral motif, distinctive high handle. *Private Collection.*

Plate 457
TEA CUP. D 3⅝in (92mm) Ht 2in (50mm).
Coalport, pattern number 830, Empire shape cup decorated with enamelled flowers and panels of elaborate pebbled and seeded gilding, with elegant high loop handle (compare Plates 487 and 488). This handle form was also used at Derby (Plate 489) and Swansea (Plate 440). *Micawber Antiques, Wingham.*

Plate 458
COFFEE CUP. D 2¹⁵⁄₁₆in (74mm) Ht 2⅞in (72mm).
Coalport, no mark, cup of Empire shape decorated inside with a dark blue ground and panels of flowers, good quality gilding, high loop handle with distinct knob inside the cup. *Patricia Ratcliffe.*

Plate 459
TEA CUP. D 3¹³⁄₁₆in (97mm) Ht 1¹⁵⁄₁₆in (49mm).
Factory unknown, pattern number 1370, cup of Empire shape, decorated with elaborate gilding and flower sprays, well modelled handle with internal upper and external lower moulded finials. *The Berthoud Collection.*

Plate 460
TEA CUP. D 3³⁄₁₆in (97mm) Ht 1¹⁵⁄₁₆in (49mm).
Factory unknown, pattern number 1342, another version of the tea cup shown in Plate 459 with twenty six vertical flutes and similar handle, decorated with a blue border above and below carelessly painted enamelled flowers. *The Berthoud Collection.*

Plate 461
TEA CUP. D 4¹⁄₁₆in (103mm) Ht 2³⁄₁₆in (55mm).
Factory unknown, no mark, Empire shape cup decorated with pink bell flowers and gilding, ring handle with top spur (see Plate 887), probably Herculaneum. *Mona & Gerald Sattin.*

Plate 462
COFFEE CUP. D 2¹⁵⁄₁₆in (74mm) Ht 2⅝in (66mm).
Factory unknown, pattern number 297, Empire shape cup contemporary with those shown in Plates 459-461 but from a different factory, decorated inside with two apricot panels and oak leaves and acorns in two shades of blue alternating with panels of enamelled flowers, handle lacking the moulded 'fan' and finials and with a weak curve to the lower support. *The Berthoud Collection.*

Plate 463
BREAKFAST CUP. D 4¹⁵/₁₆in (125mm) Ht 3in (76mm).
Rockingham, no mark, large primrose leaf moulded breakfast cup decorated with gilding to the divided crossover handle, dontil edge inside, four leaves outlined in gold. *Bruce Newmane.*

Plate 464
COFFEE CUP. D 3³/₁₆in (81mm) Ht 3³/₁₆in (81mm).
Rockingham, pattern number 655, primrose leaf moulded cup with divided handle, gilt dontil edge inside and slight embellishment to the handle. *Philip Miller.*

Plate 465
TEA CUP. D 3⅝in (92mm) Ht 2⅛in (53mm).
Ridgway, pattern number 5/3859 (c. 1850), moulded cup, the body formed of six moulded acanthus leaves, gilt edged against a dark blue ground, crossover handle with moulded leaves (see Godden (16) Plate 98). *The Berthoud Collection.*

Plate 466
COFFEE CUP. D 2¾in (69mm) Ht 2¾in (69mm).
Wedgwood, brown printed mark c. 1812-1822, vine leaf moulded cup with gilt stem and handles. *The Victoria & Albert Museum.*

Plate 467
TEA CUP. D 3¾in (95mm) Ht 2in (50mm).
Coalport, pattern number 988, on a shape called 'New Embossed' in the Coalport pattern books decorated with a dark blue ground and panels of enamelled flowers, the embossed flowers in white and gold, two handle forms occur on this shape (compare Plate 468). *Bill Dickenson, Ironbridge.*

Plate 468
COFFEE CUP. D 2⁷/₁₆in (61mm) Ht 2⅝in (66mm).
Coalport, pattern number 988, the cup of cruciform shape with alternate broad and narrow panels, the broad panels with embossed flowers on a dark blue ground and the narrow panels with enamelled flowers, alternate handle form. *Micawber Antiques, Wingham.*

Plate 469
TEA CUP. D 3¾in (95mm) Ht 2⁷⁄₁₆in (61mm).
Spode, marked SPODE and pattern number 4912 in gold (c. 1831), twelve sided cup introduced by Spode c. 1829, decorated with a cream ground, purple scale border and enamelled flowers. *The Berthoud Collection.*

Plate 470
COFFEE CUP. D 3¹⁄₁₆in (78mm) Ht 2⅞in (72mm).
Copeland and Garrett, felspar back stamp in brown and pattern number 5083, twelve sided cup usually referred to as of 'octagon' shape introduced by Spode 1829, decorated with brown printed flowers and gilding. *Alan Townsend Collection.*

Plate 471
COFFEE CUP. D 3in (76mm) Ht 2⅜in (60mm).
Davenport, puce crown mark 'Davenport, Longport, Staffordshire' and pattern number 874, twelve sided cup decorated inside with a grey border and finely enamelled flowers and gilding. *The Berthoud Collection.*

Plate 472
COFFEE CUP. D 3⅛in (79mm) Ht 2½in (63mm).
Factory unknown, pattern number 744, ribbed cup, straight sided gadrooned edge under the flared lip, decorated with a dark blue ground with musical emblems and Imari flowers, probably Machin. *The Berthoud Collection.*

Plate 473
TEA CUP. D 3¾in (95mm) Ht 2⅛in (53mm).
Minton, pattern number 171, cup with ribbed body and distinctive handle designated 'N' in the Minton shape book, decorated with a lilac ground and some gilding. Pattern numbers in the range 140-570 approximately may be found on this shape. *The Berthoud Collection.*

Plate 474
COFFEE CUP. D 3⅛in (79mm) Ht 2⅝in (66mm).
Minton, pattern number 141, cup with ribbed body and distinctive handle introduced c. 1824 and designated 'N' in the Minton shape book (see Introduction). *The Berthoud Collection.*

Plate 475
BREAKFAST CUP. D 4½in (114mm) Ht 2⅜in (66mm).
Spode, no mark, 'New Dresden' shape introduced c. 1817 (see Whiter (7) page 128) with small embossed flowers, decorated with a gilt border only, Dresden handle. *Philip Miller.*

Plate 476
COFFEE CUP. D 2¹⁵/₁₆in (74mm) Ht 2¼in (56mm).
Spode, pattern number 2527 (c. 1817), 'New Dresden' shape with small regular moulded flowers, decorated with enamel flower sprays ignoring moulding, Dresden handle. *Philip Miller.*

Plate 477
BUCKET CAN. D 2⁹/₁₆in (64mm) Ht 2¼in (56mm).
Factory unknown, no marks, tapered bucket can well potted but of a poor quality paste, with moulding very similar to Spode's New Dresden shape (Plates 475 and 476) decorated with enamelled birds and butterflies, plain loop handle. *The Victoria & Albert Museum.*

Plate 478
COFFEE CUP. D 3in (76mm) Ht 2⁹/₁₆in (64mm).
Factory unknown, no mark, lattice moulded cup of very clear translucent body, decorated with enamelled roses, Dresden handle. *The Berthoud Collection.*

Plate 479
TEA CUP. D 3¼in (82mm) Ht 2in (50mm).
Minton, unmarked but conforming to the shape designated 'E, Dresden Embossed' in the Minton shape book, decorated with a claret ground and flower sprays in a reserved panel surrounded by moulded scrolls and with a Dresden type handle. Patterns in the 1200 range may be found. *The Berthoud Collection.*

Plate 480
TEA CUP. D 3½in (89mm) Ht 2¼in (56mm).
Factory unknown, no mark, moulded cup with Dresden handle, usually attributed to Coalport on the strength of Godden (9) Plate 60 from which it differs in certain details in the moulding and a small spur on top of the handle (missing in the Coalport version) see also Smith (14) Plate 133 in which the tea cup is accompanied by a coffee can and is erroneously attributed to Coalport. *Bill Dickenson, Ironbridge.*

Plate 481
TEA CUP. D 3in (76mm) Ht 2in (50mm).
Meissen, crossed swords mark in blue, quatrefoil cup with broad panels decorated with romantic scenes in coloured enamels alternating with narrow panels of solid gilding. Solid gilt handle with curved upper and lower spurs. *The Royal Museum, Canterbury.*

Plate 482
TEA CUP. D 3⁹/₁₆in (90mm) Ht 2¼in (56mm).
Factory unknown, no mark, moulded with a honeycomb pattern, shells and flowers in a very clear translucent body, matt buff ground, pink roses and green leaves, the shells picked out in purple (Philip Miller has recorded a sucrier with similar moulding marked AB/34), Dresden type handle. *The Berthoud Collection.*

Plate 483
TEA CUP. D 3⁷/₁₆in (87mm) Ht 2³/₁₆in (55mm).
New Hall, no mark, bone china cup with basket weave moulding, decorated with a blue band inside and enamel flowers outside, Dresden type handle. *City Museum & Art Gallery, Stoke-on-Trent.*

Plate 484
COFFEE CUP. D 3¹/₁₆in (78mm) Ht 2⅜in (60mm).
New Hall c. 1825, no mark, bone china cup of basic London shape with basket weave pattern, decorated with a blue border and enamelled flowers, patterns between 1944 and 2050 have been recorded, Dresden type handle. *The Berthoud Collection.*

Plate 485
TEA CUP. D 3⅞in (98mm) Ht 1¹³/₁₆in (46mm).
Alcock, pattern number 4545 c. 1835, moulded cup with thirty two pronounced ribs and four water lily leaves, decorated in blue and gold, modified Dresden type handle. *Dr. Geoffrey & Alma Barnes Collection.*

Plate 486
COFFEE CUP. D 3³/₁₆in (81mm) Ht 2⅜in (60mm).
Alcock, pattern number 4627 c. 1835, cup of similar moulding to that shown in Plate 485, decorated with three green panels with pale yellow hatched panels and leaves, modified Dresden type handle. *Private Collection.*

Plate 487
TEA CUP. D 3⅝in (92mm) Ht 2in (50mm).
Coalport, no mark, shallow cup decorated with a blue ground, elaborate gilding, enamelled flowers in two reserved panels, high loop handle. *Bill Dickenson, Ironbridge.*

Plate 488
COFFEE CUP. D 3in (76mm) Ht 2in (50mm).
Coalport, no mark, straight sided cup with high loop handle, decorated with a dark blue ground and gilt cartouches containing typical sprays of enamelled flowers. *Mercury Antiques.*

Plate 489
BREAKFAST CUP. D 4¼in (107) Ht 2⁷⁄₁₆in (61mm).
Derby, red baton mark, Paris flute cup decorated with a gold border with blue dots, high loop handle (compare Plates 439-442). *The Berthoud Collection.*

Plate 490
COFFEE CUP. D 3¼in (82mm) Ht 2⅝in (66mm).
Grainger, marked S. Hadley (probably an outside decorator), gadroon edged cup decorated with a pink ground with square yellow panel containing a flower spray, raised gilt spots, high loop handle with feathered top. An alternative form has a moulded cartouche. *Private Collection.*

Plate 491
TEA CUP. 3¹³⁄₁₆in (97mm) Ht 2⁵⁄₁₆in (58mm).
Ridgway, pattern number 2/1836 c. 1825, gadroon edged cup with pedestal foot, decorated inside and out with small brown flowers, high loop handle. *The Berthoud Collection.*

Plate 492
COFFEE CUP. D 3⅛in (79mm) Ht 3in (76mm).
Ridgway, no mark, c. 1825, gadroon edged cup with pedestal foot, decorated inside and out with printed and enamelled brown flowers, high loop handle. *The Berthoud Collection.*

Plate 493
TEA CUP. D 3⅞in (98mm) Ht 1¾in (44mm).
Spode, pattern number 3710, Etruscan shape cup with earlier angular form of handle, decorated with a Japanese vase pattern (see Whiter (7) page 128 and Plate 237). *The Berthoud Collection.*

Plate 494
TEA CUP. D 3¾in (95mm) Ht 1⅞in (48mm).
Factory unknown, no mark, Etruscan shape cup decorated with a Japanese floral pattern in blue, orange, green and gold with typical handle profile but unusually narrow lower attachment. Probably Charles Bourne. *Christopher May.*

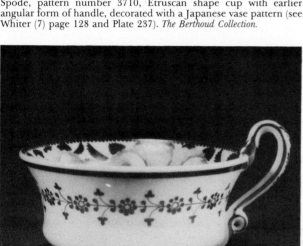

Plate 495
TEA CUP. D 3⅞in (98mm) Ht 2in (50mm).
Spode, marked SPODE and pattern number 3614 in red, Etruscan shape cup decorated with pairs of roses with gilt leaves, the well modelled handle in the form of a serpent (replacing the earlier angular version, Plate 493) and probably not used elsewhere. *The Berthoud Collection.*

Plate 496
COFFEE CUP. D 2¹⁵⁄₁₆in (74mm) Ht 2⁹⁄₁₆in (64mm).
Spode, marked SPODE and pattern number 3631 in red, Etruscan shape cup decorated inside with a blue and orange Imari pattern, serpent handle (see Whiter (7) page 128). *The Berthoud Collection.*

Plate 497
TEA CUP. D 3¼in (82mm) Ht 1¾in (44mm).
H. & R. Daniel, pattern number 3863, shallow Etruscan cup decorated with enamelled flowers, gilt dontil edge and seeded panels (see Berthoud (17) Plate 9). *The Berthoud Collection.*

Plate 498
COFFEE CUP. D 3in (76mm) Ht 2⅝in (66mm).
H. & R. Daniel, pattern number 3862, Etruscan shape cup decorated with green and yellow panels and single roses and buttercups, probably by William Pollard (see Berthoud (17) Plate 9). *The Berthoud Collection.*

Plate 499
TEA CUP. D 4in (101mm) Ht 2¹⁄₁₆in (52mm).
Coalport, no mark, Etruscan shape with angular handle, the lower attachment joining just below the bulge, decorated with pairs of roses and gilt leaves. *Private Collection.*

Plate 500
COFFEE CUP. D 3⁵⁄₁₆in (84mm) Ht 2¾in (69mm).
Factory unknown, no mark, heavy Etruscan shape decorated with a crude version of Daniel's pattern 3859. *The Berthoud Collection.*

Plate 501
TEA CUP. D 3¹³⁄₁₆in (97mm) Ht 1⅞in (48mm).
Coalport, no mark, Etruscan shape cup with angular handle, the lower support joining the cup on and below the bulge, decorated with a simulated scale blue ground and enamelled birds in gilt cartouches. Gilding includes the five gold rings motif also used by Minton and Davenport. *The Berthoud Collection.*

Plate 502
COFFEE CUP. D 3in (76mm) Ht 2⅝in (66mm).
Coalport, no mark, Etruscan shape with rather small, wide angled handle, decorated inside with light and dark blue bell flowers and gilding. *The Berthoud Collection.*

Plate 503
TEA CUP. D 3¹³⁄₁₆in (97mm) Ht 2in (50mm).
Davenport, brown wreath mark and pattern number 776, of Etruscan shape, the lower member joining the cup below the bulge, decorated inside with a band of gilt grapes and green vine leaves. *The Berthoud Collection.*

Plate 504
COFFEE CUP. D 3¹⁄₁₆in (78mm) Ht 2⁵⁄₁₆in (58mm).
Davenport, brown wreath mark, of broad bodied Etruscan shape with upturned handle, decorated inside with single roses and gilt leaves. *Private Collection.*

Plate 505
BREAKFAST CUP. D 4¼in (107mm) Ht 2¹/₁₆in (52mm).
Worcester, Flight Barr & Barr period impressed crown and FBB, large cup of greyish body, decorated with a dark blue ground and panels of Japan style flowers, large handle with lower attachment joining below the bulge. *The Berthoud Collection.*

Plate 506
COFFEE CUP. D 3¼in (82mm) Ht 2¹³/₁₆in (71mm).
Worcester, Flight Barr & Barr period, impressed crown and FBB mark, matching coffee cup to the cup shown in Plate 505, the handle with the lower attachment joining the cup above the bulge. *Jean Sewell Antiques.*

Plate 507
SMALL TEA CUP. D 3¼in (82mm) Ht 1¹/₁₆in (27mm).
Davenport, blue printed mark, earthenware Etruscan cup with blue printed pattern inside and out. *The Berthoud Collection.*

Plate 508
COFFEE CUP. D 3in (76mm) Ht 2⁵/₁₆in (58mm).
Factory unknown, no mark, cup of very light weight body decorated with pink roses and blue convolvuli, disproportionately large handle. *The Berthoud Collection.*

Plate 509
TEA CUP. D 3¾in (95mm) Ht 2¼in (56mm).
Rockingham, pattern number 723, Etruscan shape cup of rather heavy design decorated with a band of pale blue and three pink roses inside and enamelled landscapes outside, characteristic rather heavy handle (see Rice (18) Plate 94). *The Berthoud Collection.*

Plate 510
COFFEE CUP. D 3½in (89mm) Ht 2⅝in (66mm).
Rockingham, pattern 636, Etruscan shape cup decorated with a blue underglaze printed pattern of Chinese figures embellished with orange and gilt leaves (pattern illustrated Rice (18) Plate 90). *The Berthoud Collection.*

Plate 511
COFFEE CUP. D 3¹/₁₆in (78mm) Ht 2¹¹/₁₆in (68mm).
Rockingham, puce griffin mark on the saucer, pattern number 728, cup of unusual shape decorated with a blue transfer printed pattern with gilding, handle in a form more usually found on Rockingham Etruscan cups. *Bruce Newmane.*

Plate 512
COFFEE CUP. D 3¹/₁₆in (78mm) Ht 2¹³/₁₆in (71mm).
Rockingham, pattern number 743, bucket shaped cup decorated with a green ground with enamelled shells by Speight in a reserved panel, from a service made for the Canadian market (see Rice (18) Plate 101). *Bruce Newmane.*

Plate 513
TEA CUP. D 3¾in (95mm) Ht 2in (50mm).
Davenport, brown wreath mark and pattern number 707, Etruscan shape decorated with small enamelled flower sprays and with characteristic upward curved handle. *Private Collection.*

Plate 514
TEA CUP. D 4⅛in (104mm) Ht 1½in (38mm).
Davenport, purple wreath mark, of flattened Etruscan shape and sharply upturned handle, embossed wreath and flowers moulding, decorated with a gilt border inside and with single enamelled flowers. *Private Collection.*

Plate 515
TEA CUP. D 3⅝in (92mm) Ht 2½in (63mm).
Coalport, the saucer marked with the Royal Society of Arts Felspar back stamp, a rare example of Coalport tea wares with palm leaf and wreath moulding, probably derived from Sèvres by way of Nantgarw (Godden (9) Plate 154 illustrates a teapot). *Bruce Newmane.*

Plate 516
TEA CUP. D 3¹¹/₁₆in (94mm) Ht 2¹/₁₆in (52mm).
Attributed to Coalport, no mark, scallop edged cup with palm leaf and wreath moulding, decorated with enamelled flowers. *M. Jacobs Antiques, Tenterden, Kent.*

Plate 517
TEA CUP. D 3¼in (82mm) Ht 2in (50mm).
Factory unknown, pattern number 1231, Etruscan shape cup decorated with a dark blue ground colour, enamelled flowers and gilding. *Christopher May.*

Plate 518
COFFEE CUP. D 2⅞in (72mm) Ht 2¾in (69mm).
Factory unknown, pattern 841, coffee cup from the same factory as the cup shown in Plate 517, decorated with a blue ground and gilding and a figure of Dr. Syntax drinking a yard of ale. *Private Collection.*

Plate 519
TEA CUP. D 3¹³⁄₁₆in (97mm) Ht 2in (50mm).
Factory unknown, no mark, Etruscan shape cup decorated inside with a dark blue ground and a version of Ridgway's shell pattern 1052 (see Plate 530 and Godden (16) Plate 42). *The Victoria & Albert Museum.*

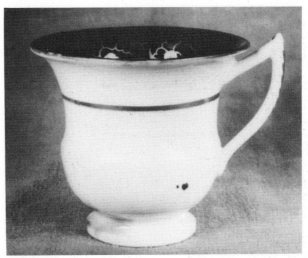

Plate 520
COFFEE CUP. D 2⅞in (72mm) Ht 2½in (63mm).
Coalport, no mark, narrow bell-shaped cup with flared rim, the handle a modified version of the Etruscan with the lower attachment forming an ogee curve, decorated inside with a dark blue ground, a yellow pineapple and a large leaf, with enamelled flowers in the centre. *Liz Jackson Antiques.*

Plate 521
TEA CUP. D 3½in (89mm) Ht 2¼in (56mm).
Factory unknown, pattern number 2901, Etruscan shape cup decorated with a pattern of roses and gilding, sharply upturned handle, probably New Hall. *Philip Miller.*

Plate 522
COFFEE CUP. D 2⅞in (72mm) Ht 2⁵⁄₁₆in (58mm).
Factory unknown, pattern number 2784, coffee cup of similar shape to the tea cup shown in Plate 521, decorated with a gilt pattern of grey 'bosses', sharply upturned handle, probably New Hall. *Philip Miller*

Plate 523
TEA CUP. D 3⅝in (92mm) Ht 2½in (63mm).
Factory unknown, no mark, Etruscan shape cup decorated with a pattern of enamelled flower sprays and gilding with dontil border and seeded panels (similar to Daniel's pattern 3863), very sharply upturned weak handle. *The Berthoud Collection.*

Plate 524
COFFEE CUP. D 2⅞in (72mm) Ht 2¼in (56mm).
Factory unknown, pattern number 2802 in gold, Etruscan cup decorated with a pattern of flowers and gilding with large dontil border and seeded panels (similar to Daniel's pattern 3863) good translucency, strongly formed handle. *The Berthoud Collection.*

Plate 525
TEA CUP. D 3¾in (95mm) Ht 2¼in (56mm).
Spode, impressed 6 and pattern 4148 in red, bell-shaped cup (introduced c. 1820 see Whiter (7) page 128), decorated with a fawn ground and gilt sprays, complex handle, examples may be found bearing Daniel patterns and numbers. *Dover Street Antiques, Canterbury.*

Plate 526
COFFEE CUP. D 3¼in (82mm) Ht 2¹¹⁄₁₆in (68mm).
Spode, marked SPODE and pattern number 3902, bell-shaped cup decorated with an apricot border and gilding, complex handle. *Jean Sewell Antiques.*

Plate 527
COFFEE CUP. D 3⅝in (92mm) Ht 3¹³⁄₁₆in (97mm).
Grainger, marked 565X in gold, decorated inside with a dark blue ground and enamelled flowers, high handle with graded gilt dots. *City Museum & Art Gallery, Stoke-on-Trent.*

Plate 528
COFFEE CUP. D 3¾in (95mm) Ht 2¾in (69mm).
Factory unknown, pattern number 529, moulded edge cup decorated inside with pale grey panels and enamelled flowers, unusual twisted handle. *The Berthoud Collection.*

Plate 529
TEA CUP. D 3¹¹/₁₆in (94mm) Ht 1¹³/₁₆in (46mm).
Ridgway, pattern number 2/1063, scallop edged cup decorated with flowers in the centre, narrow blue border and gilding, gilt old English handle with high point (compare Coalport Plate 531). *G.A. Godden.*

Plate 530
COFFEE CUP. D 3⅛in (79mm) Ht 2½in (63mm).
Ridgway, pattern number 2/1070, scallop edged cup with vertical ribbing, decorated with a dark blue ground with gilt shells and a scalloped cartouche of flowers (see Plate 519), this pattern is 1052 on Ridgway dessert wares (see Godden (16) Plate 42). *Mona & Gerald Sattin.*

Plate 531
TEA CUP. D 3½in (89mm) Ht 1⅞in (48mm).
Coalport, pattern number 830, scallop edged cup similar to those from the Ridgway, Rockingham and other factories, decorated with enamelled flowers and panels of elaborate pebbled and seeded gilding. *Jean Sewell Antiques.*

Plate 532
COFFEE CUP. D 3in (76mm) Ht 2½in (63mm).
Coalport, pattern number 2/147, scallop edged cup with vertical ribbing, decorated inside with a band of rich blue with gilt shells and enamelled flowers. *Private Collection.*

Plate 533
TEA CUP. D 3¹¹/₁₆in (94mm) Ht 2in (50mm).
Davenport, brown wreath mark, scallop edged cup of a rare shape more commonly associated with Ridgway, decorated with single flowers (see Lockett (6) Plate 83 (i). *Philip Miller.*

Plate 534
TEA CUP. D 3¹/₁₆in (78mm) Ht 2¾in (69mm).
Rockingham, puce griffin mark on the saucer and pattern number 781, c. 1833-41 fluted cup of unusual form decorated with leaves in a thick green enamel, old English handle set slightly below the rim (compare Plates 539 and 540). *Bruce Newmane.*

Plate 535
TEA CUP. D 3¹³/₁₆in (97mm) Ht 1¹⁵/₁₆in (49mm).
Factory A (see Introduction) pattern number 1467, scallop edged cup decorated inside with a dark blue ground with spiral gilding, deep caramel panels and pink fans, old English handle with straight back, pointed finial and gilt top. *The Berthoud Collection.*

Plate 536
COFFEE CUP. D 3⅜in (86mm) Ht 2⁷/₁₆in (61mm).
Factory A (see Introduction) pattern number 1612, decorated with a blue band inside and gilding, flat topped handle gilded as in Plate 535, but from a service with cups of similar shape to Spode's '4643' shape (see Plates 693 and 695). *Bill Dickenson, Ironbridge.*

Plate 537
TEA CUP. D 3⅝in (92mm) Ht 1¹⁵/₁₆in (49mm).
Factory unknown, pattern number 3013, scallop edged cup decorated with a band of blue, hatched gilding and enamelled peasant figures, light weight body, rather thin handle angled from the cup, possibly New Hall. *G.A. Godden.*

Plate 538
COFFEE CUP. D 3¹/₁₆in (78mm) Ht 2⅜in (60mm).
Factory unknown, pattern 2901, scallop edged cup decorated with two pairs of enamelled roses and gilding, thinly potted handle set at an angle from the cup, possibly New Hall. *Philip Miller.*

Plate 539
TEA CUP. D 4in (101mm) Ht 2¼in (56mm).
Rockingham, pattern number 613, scallop edged cup decorated with a blue ground and yellow leaves, trios in this shape were often accompanied by a cup plate, thickly potted handle often touching the rim of the cup (compare Plates 535 and 537). *Bruce Newmane.*

Plate 540
COFFEE CUP. D 3⁷/₁₆in (87mm) Ht 2¾in (69mm).
Rockingham, no mark, scallop edged cup decorated inside with crudely painted flowers and gilding, handle typically set well below the rim (see Rice (18) Plate 90). *City Museum & Art Gallery, Stoke-on-Trent.*

Plate 541
COFFEE CUP. D 3¹⁄₁₆in (78mm) Ht 2⁹⁄₁₆in (64mm).
Ridgway, no mark, scallop edged cup with vertical ribbing, decorated with printed and enamelled orange flowers. *The Berthoud Collection.*

Plate 542
COFFEE CUP. D 3in (76mm) Ht 2⅜in (60mm).
Coalport, no mark, scallop edged cup with vertical ribbing, decorated with a pink print of flowers and butterflies. This print also occurs in other colours, sometimes with the pattern number 2/310 (see Plate 633). *Private Collection.*

Plate 543
TEA CUP. D 3¾in (95mm) Ht 2¹⁄₁₆in (52mm).
Factory unknown, pattern number 75, scallop edged cup decorated with two internal blue panels and roses with gilt leaves, rather weak old English handle. *Private Collection.*

Plate 544
COFFEE CUP. D 3⅛in (79mm) Ht 2⁷⁄₁₆in (61mm).
Charles Bourne, marked CB/675, probably representing a transition between the London shape and scallop edged cup (in this case with a plain edge), decorated with a blue ground and enamelled flower sprays, rather weak old English handle. *The Berthoud Collection.*

Plate 545
COFFEE CUP. D 3¹⁄₁₆in (78mm) Ht 2⁷⁄₁₆in (61mm).
Factory unknown, pattern number 1291 in blue, scallop edged cup decorated with a yellow band inside and a flower spray in the bottom. Straight old English handle of Factory A type (compare Plates 535 and 536) with gilt thumb rest. *The Berthoud Collection.*

Plate 546
COFFEE CUP. D 2¹³⁄₁₆in (71mm) Ht 2⅜in (60mm).
Factory unknown, scallop edged cup decorated with a blue transfer printed 'Broseley' pattern and inner border, vertical old English handle with pointed thumb rest. *The Berthoud Collection.*

Plate 547
TEA CUP. D 2¹⁵/₁₆in (74mm) Ht 2¹¹/₁₆in (68mm).
Gardners (Moscow), standard orange printed mark, small Pembroke cup decorated with a blue ground, fawn leaves and enamelled flowers. *The Berthoud Collection.*

Plate 548
TEA CUP. D 3⁹/₁₆in (90mm) Ht 2in (50mm).
Coalport, pattern number 966, the cup and handle very similar to Spode's Pembroke shape (Plates 549 and 551), but with rather irregularly formed gadrooned edge, decorated with enamelled flowers and pebble gilding. *The Berthoud Collection.*

Plate 549
TEA CUP. D 3¹¹/₁₆in (94mm) Ht 2in (50mm).
Spode, X incised and pattern number 4349 in orange, Spode's Pembroke shape introduced c. 1827 (see Whiter (7) page 129) in both plain and moulded form but not gadrooned as at Coalport (Plate 548), handle with prominent 'tongue'. *The Berthoud Collection.*

Plate 550
COFFEE CUP. D 2⁹/₁₆in (64mm) Ht 2⅞in (72mm).
Spode, marked SPODE in red and pattern number 4587, Pembroke plain shape cup with slightly flared lip, decorated with gilt scrolls and purple enamel, handle with flattened 'tongue'. *Jean Sewell Antiques.*

Plate 551
TEA CUP. D 3¾in (95mm) Ht 2⅛in (53mm).
Spode, impressed X and pattern number 4448 the saucer marked SPODE, Pembroke embossed shape with a wavy edge decorated with a dark blue moulded cartouche and elaborate gilding, handle with rudimentary 'tongue'. *Gus Brain Antiques.*

Plate 552
COFFEE CUP. D 2⁹/₁₆in (64mm) Ht 2⅞in (72mm).
Spode, no mark, Pembroke embossed shape decorated with a grey bat print within a moulded cartouche and with printed flowers inside, handle with rudimentary 'tongue'. *Jean Sewell Antiques.*

Plate 553
TEA CUP. D 3¹¹/₁₆in (94mm) Ht 2⅛in (53mm).
H. & R. Daniel, no mark, First Gadroon shape (see Berthoud (17)
Plate 12), of basic London shape with wavy edge and external
gadrooning decorated with red leaves and gilt barley ears, well
modelled scroll handle. *The Berthoud Collection.*

Plate 554
TEA CUP. D 3⁹/₁₆in (90mm) Ht 2¼in (56mm).
Spode, pattern number 4308, introduced c. 1822, of basic London
shape with concave sides and external gadrooning, decorated inside
with blue and buff panels and elaborate gilding, distinctive handle
not used elsewhere. *The Berthoud Collection.*

Plate 555
COFFEE CUP. D 3in (76mm) Ht 2½in (63mm).
H. & R. Daniel, no mark, First Gadroon shape with straight sides and
external gadrooning, decorated with gilt line only, tightly modelled
handle (compare Davenport Plate 558). *Christopher May.*

Plate 556
COFFEE CAN. D 2¾in (69mm) Ht 2¾in (69mm).
H. & R. Daniel, no mark, extremely rare example of a Daniel coffee
can with gadrooned edge and tightly modelled handle looking
disproportionately small, decorated with a blue printed floral pattern
inside and out. *Betty Reed.*

Plate 557
LARGE TEA CUP. D 3¾in (95mm) Ht 2¼in (56mm).
Worcester, Flight Barr & Barr period impressed crown and FBB mark,
cup of basic London shape with solid gilt external gadrooning
reintroduced at Worcester c. 1816, decorated with red flowers and
brown leaves, typical handle. *The Berthoud Collection.*

Plate 558
COFFEE CUP. D 3¹/₁₆in (78mm) Ht 2⁷/₁₆in (61mm).
Davenport, brown wreath mark and pattern number 784, of unusual
shape with gadrooned edge, similar to H. & R. Daniel's First Gadroon
shape but with the handle of oval form, decorated with gilding only
(compare Plates 553, 555 and 556). *The Berthoud Collection.*

Plate 559
TEA CUP. D 4in (101mm) Ht 1¹³/₁₆in (46mm).
H. & R. Daniel, saucer marked H. & R. Daniel in puce script, cup of Second Gadroon shape with the gadrooning inside a widely flared lip, decorated with a green ground and buff ribbons, flower baskets in panels and flowers in the centre. *The Berthoud Collection.*

Plate 560
TEA CUP. D 4in (101mm) Ht 1⅞in (48mm).
Coalport, standard Coalport mark of c. 1891-1939 and pattern number 5772, an extremely accurate copy of the cup shown in Plate 559 with blue ground decoration (see also Plates 817 and 818). *Bill Dickenson, Ironbridge.*

Plate 561
TEA CUP. D 4in (101mm) Ht 1¾in (44mm).
H. & R. Daniel, pattern number 4237, cup of Daniel's Second Gadroon basic shape but in a rare form without the gadrooned moulding, decorated with enamelled birds and gilt vine leaves, a pattern also to be found on tea wares in the Shrewsbury shape. *The Berthoud Collection.*

Plate 562
TEA CUP. D 4⅛in (104mm) Ht 2¹/₁₆in (52mm).
Minton, pattern number N4239, a fairly common shape with embossed leaves on the flared rim and high D handle, shown in the Minton shape book as shape 'Q', decorated with a grey ground and printed and enamelled flowers. *Micawber Antiques, Wingham, Kent.*

Plate 563
TEA CUP. D 4⅛in (104mm) Ht 2¼in (56mm).
Chamberlain, no mark, with moulded rim similar to H. & R. Daniel's 'Shell' border and feathered handle, the moulding picked out in blue (see Berthoud (17) Plate 70 for a plate with similar moulded border), Decorated with printed and enamelled flowers. *The Berthoud Collection.*

Plate 564
COFFEE CUP. D 3³/₁₆in (81mm) Ht 3in (76mm).
Chamberlain, no mark, moulded edge cup with D handle, decorated inside only with a garter in black and motto 'Grata Sume Manu'. *The Dyson Perrins Museum, Worcester.*

Plate 565
TEA CUP. D 3⅞in (98mm) Ht 2in (50mm).
H. & R. Daniel, printed mark of the Prince of Wales feathers, 'Peacock' and 'D', earthenware cup of plain edged shape (compare Plates 566 and 593) decorated with a green printed pattern inside and out (see Berthoud (17) Plates 102 and 135(h)). *The Berthoud Collection.*

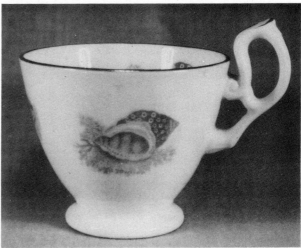

Plate 566
COFFEE CUP. D 3⅛in (53mm) Ht 2½in (63mm).
H. & R. Daniel, no mark, bone china cup of Plain shape (see Berthoud (17) Plates 55 and 56) decorated with a pink bat print of shells, distinctive handle. *The Berthoud Collection.*

Plate 567
TEA CUP. D 3¼in (32mm) Ht 2⅜in (60mm).
Factory C as yet unidentified (see Introduction), pattern number 22, ribbed cup on a pedestal foot with moulded border and unique crested handle, pattern numbers are usually low. *The Berthoud Collection.*

Plate 568
COFFEE CUP. D 3³⁄₁₆in (81mm) Ht 2¾in (69mm).
Factory C, as yet unidentified, ribbed cup on a pedestal foot with moulded border, decorated inside with a buff ground, green daisies and gilding. *Liz Jackson Antiques.*

Plate 569
TEA CUP. D 3¹¹⁄₁₆in (94mm) Ht 2in (50mm).
H. & R. Daniel, pattern number 4582, cup of Daniel's Plain shape, variation B with complex moulded handle, decorated with enamelled birds and seeded and hatched gilding. *Dr. Geoffrey & Alma Barnes Collection.*

Plate 570
COFFEE CUP. D 3⅛in (79mm) Ht 2½in (63mm).
H. & R. Daniel, no mark, cup of Daniel's Plain shape variation B with complex moulded handle, simply decorated with bands of gilding, a pattern also to be found on variation A in this shape. *Philip Miller.*

Plate 571
TEA CUP. D 3⅞in (98mm) Ht 2⁹⁄₁₆in (64mm).
H. & R. Daniel, pattern number 4413, cup of Daniel's C-Scroll shape with, delicately moulded handle and three flower feet joined by moulded leaves and stems (see Berthoud (17) page 77 and Plate 61), decorated with pink vine leaves and gilding. *The Berthoud Collection.*

Plate 572
COFFEE CUP. D 3³⁄₁₆in (81mm) Ht 2⅞in (72mm).
H. & R. Daniel, pattern number 4630, cup of Daniel's Mayflower shape with delicately moulded handle, moulded scrolls forming cartouches in a field of moulded florets, decorated with panels of enamelled flowers with bright green leaves and with the florets picked out in pale blue. *Micawber Antiques, Wingham, Kent.*

Plate 573
TEA CUP. D 3⅝in (92mm) Ht 2⅛in (53mm).
Chamberlain, no mark, cup of similar shape and moulding to the Coalport cup shown in Plate 574 but with a Worcester type handle (compare Plates 279 and 281), decorated with a blue ground and gilding. *The Berthoud Collection.*

Plate 574
TEA CUP. D 3⁹⁄₁₆in (90mm) Ht 2⅛in (53mm).
Coalport, no mark, scallop edged cup with six vertical ribs, band of gadrooning and moulded acanthus leaves below, large kicked loop handle (compare Chamberlain Plate 573). *The Berthoud Collection.*

Plate 575
COFFEE CUP. D 2⅞in (72mm) Ht 2¾in (69mm).
H. & R. Daniel, pattern number 4415, C-Scroll shape (see Berthoud (17) Plates 59-61), with spiral moulded base, three flower feet and moulded handle, decorated with a blue ground, three pink single roses and flower sprays, elaborate gilding. *Phillips of Chester.*

Plate 576
COFFEE CUP. D 3¹⁄₁₆in (78mm) Ht 2⅝in (66mm).
Chamberlain, no mark, but decorated with Chamberlain's pattern 1030 (see Plates 643 and 644), the cup with moulded base similar to a Coalport shape (Plate 574) but with a handle more typical of the Worcester factories, decorated with a dark blue ground and enamelled flowers. *The Berthoud Collection.*

Plate 577
TEA CUP. D 3¾in (95mm) Ht 2⅛in (53mm).
H. & R. Daniel, pattern number 4787, cup of Daniel's Shell shape variation A with standard shell moulded border and delicately modelled handle (see Berthoud (17) Plate 69a), decorated with a deep pink ground and yellow 'kidney' panels with delicate gilding. *The Berthoud Collection.*

Plate 578
TEA CUP. D 3¹⁵/₁₆in (100mm) Ht 2⅛in (53mm).
H. & R. Daniel, pattern number 5319, cup of Daniel's Shell shape variation B (see Berthoud (17) Plate 69b) with the standard shell border moulded inside the flared lip, the handle rather more heavily modelled than in variation A (Plate 577). *The Berthoud Collection.*

Plate 579
COFFEE CUP. D 3⁵/₁₆in (84mm) Ht 2¾in (69mm).
H. & R. Daniel, pattern number 5241, cup of Daniel's Shell shape variation B, decorated inside with a rose pattern in green monochrome and with green sprays outside. *The Berthoud Collection.*

Plate 580
COFFEE CUP. D 3⅜in (86mm) Ht 2¾in (69mm).
Factory unknown, pedestal footed cup with moulded flared lip decorated with a green version of Daniel's pattern 5319 (Plate 578) the handle approximating to Daniel's Shell variation B (Plate 579) probably made as a replacement. *The Berthoud Collection.*

Plate 581
TEA CUP. D4¹/₁₆in (103mm) Ht 2¼in (56mm).
Factory unknown, no mark, cup with pedestal foot and flared lip, probably made as a replacement for a cup of Daniel's Shell Variation B (compare plate 578), decorated with a copy of a Daniel pattern with a green ground and gilding. *The Berthoud Collection.*

Plate 582
TEA CUP. D 4⅛in (104mm) Ht 2in (50mm).
Grainger, moulded edge cup decorated with a turquoise ground colour and two panels of enamelled flowers, handle of similar shape to those in Plates 577-581. *The Dyson Perrins Museum, Worcester.*

Plate 583
TEA CUP. D 3⁹⁄₁₆in (90mm) Ht 2in (50mm).
H. & R. Daniel, no mark, cup of Daniel's Ribbed shape variation B, with scalloped unmoulded order and standard handle (see Berthoud (17) Page 81 and Plate 76), decorated with blue and yellow ground colours and elaborate gilding. *The Berthoud Collection.*

Plate 584
COFFEE CUP. D 3⅛in (79mm) Ht 2½in (63mm).
H. & R. Daniel, pattern number 4822, cup of Daniel's Ribbed shape variation A with moulded border and standard handle (see Berthoud (17) Plate 75), decorated with a pink ground and gilding and with three flower sprays inside. *Micawber Antiques, Wingham.*

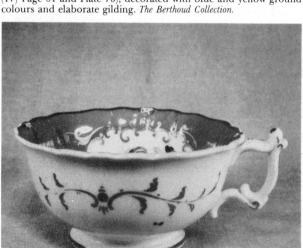

Plate 585
TEA CUP. D 4in (101mm) Ht 2⅛in (53mm).
H. & R. Daniel, no mark, cup of Daniel's Ribbed shape variation D with flared lip, the ribs placed internally and with variant handle (see Berthoud (17) Plate 79), decorated inside with a green ground and single flowers in reserved panels. *The Berthoud Collection.*

Plate 586
COFFEE CUP. D 3⅜in (86mm) Ht 2¹¹⁄₁₆in (68mm).
H. & R. Daniel, pattern number 5055, cup of Daniel's Ribbed shape variation D with internal moulded border and handle formed of three scrolls (see Berthoud (17) Page 80 and Plate 77), decorated with green panels and enamel flowers. *The Berthoud Collection.*

Plate 587
COFFEE CUP. D 3⅜in (86mm) Ht 2⅛in (53mm).
Probably Alcock, pattern number 3651, cup with five pairs of ribs to the upper part, decorated internally with a dark blue ground and gilt sprays. *The Berthoud Collection.*

Plate 588
COFFEE CUP. D 3⁷⁄₁₆in (61mm) Ht 2⅜in (60mm).
Factory unknown, pattern number 392, of similar form to that shown in Plate 587 but smaller and with shorter ribs and less well formed handle, decorated inside with a dark blue ground, gilt vine leaves and grapes. *The Berthoud Collection.*

Plate 589
TEA CUP. D 3⅝in (92mm) 2in (50mm).
Coalport (Coalbrookdale) marked CD in pale blue, octagonal cup with slightly deckled edge decorated with green leaves and gilding and with applied moulded flowers decorated in enamelled colours. *Mona & Gerald Sattin.*

Plate 590
TEA CUP. D 3⅝in (92mm) Ht 2¼in (56mm).
Factory unknown, no mark, (see Plates 591 and 592), with external gadroon border and large D shaped handle, decorated with a passable imitation of Daniel's pattern 3913 (see Berthoud (17) Colour Plate A(ii)) probably made as a replacement. *The Berthoud Collection.*

Plate 591
TEA CUP. D 4⁵⁄₁₆in (109mm) Ht 2¹⁄₁₆in (52mm).
Factory unknown, no mark, bell shaped cup on pedestal foot with large D handle, decorated inside with a grey scalloped border and with green five petalled flowers. *The Berthoud Collection.*

Plate 592
COFFEE CUP. D 3⅝in (92mm) Ht 2⅝in (66mm).
Factory unknown, pattern number 550, bell shaped cup from the same factory as that shown in Plate 591 (pattern numbers 297 and 397 have been recorded on similar cups) decorated with a green band and yellow bars. *The Berthoud Collection.*

Plate 593
TEA CUP. D 3¾in (95mm) Ht 2¹⁄₁₆in (52mm).
H. & R. Daniel, pattern number 4677, cup of Daniel's Plain shape variation A with standard D shaped handle (see Berthoud (17) page 76 and Plates 55 and 56), decorated inside with a broad band of yellow overpainted with pink flowers and grey leaves. *Micawber Antiques, Wingham, Kent.*

Plate 594
COFFEE CUP. D 3⁷⁄₁₆in (87mm) Ht 2⅝in (66mm).
H. & R. Daniel, pattern number 4342, Daniel's Second Gadroon shape with gadrooning inside the flared lip, decorated inside and out with pink flowers and brown leaves, high D handle. *The Berthoud Collection.*

Plate 595
TEA CUP. D 4in (101mm) Ht 2³⁄₁₆in (55mm).
Minton, pattern number 692, with flared lip gadrooned on the inside, designated 'K' in the Minton shape book (probably erroneously, see Introduction), decorated with pink and yellow panels and fine gilding. Pattern numbers in the range 560-700 may be found. *The Berthoud Collection.*

Plate 596
TEA CUP. D 4in (101mm) Ht 2in (50mm).
Factory unknown, unmarked and of similar basic shape to the cup shown in Plate 595, with similar handle but with plain edge and no gadrooning, decorated with a simple pattern of enamelled flower sprays. Possibly Minton. *Dover Street Antiques, Canterbury.*

Plate 597
TEA CUP. D 4in (101mm) Ht 2⅛in (53mm).
Derby, red baton mark, gadrooned edge cup with flared lip, of similar basic shape to that shown in Plate 595 but with the top spur facing away from the cup, decorated with a blue and orange Imari pattern. *The Berthoud Collection.*

Plate 598
TEA CUP. D 4in (101mm) Ht 2³⁄₁₆in (55mm).
Grainger, pattern 385x, moulded edge cup with ring and spur handle, decorated with a grey printed pattern, enamelled flowers and gilding (compare Plate 771). *The Dyson Perrins Museum, Worcester.*

Plate 599
COFFEE CUP. D 2⅜in (60mm) Ht 2¾in (69mm).
Grainger, pattern number 1996, ring and spur handle, well formed with a small flower at the junction between the ring and the lower support, decorated inside with a colourful Imari pattern. *Private Collection.*

Plate 600
COFFEE CUP. D 3⅛in (79mm) Ht 2½in (63mm).
Copeland and Garrett, crown and circle mark in green, cup of similar basic shape to that shown in Plate 710, but with the handle copying Grainger (Plates 599 and 771) and with Grainger's bead and flower moulding simulated in gilding, decorated with a maroon ground, possibly made as a replacement. *The Berthoud Collection.*

Plate 601
TEA CUP. D 4¹/₁₆in (103mm) Ht 2¹/₁₆in (52mm).
H. & R. Daniel, pattern number 4250, cup of Daniel's Shrewsbury shape (see Berthoud (17) page 75 and Plate 34), richly decorated with a dark blue ground with enamelled birds in oval panels and fine gilding. *The Berthoud Collection.*

Plate 602
COFFEE CUP. D 3½in (89mm) Ht 2¹³/₁₆in (71mm).
H. & R. Daniel, pattern number 4251, cup of Daniel's Shrewsbury shape decorated with a blue ground inside with pale yellow anthemion and enamelled flowers in the centre, D handle with top spur. *The Berthoud Collection.*

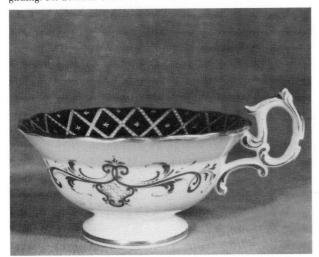

Plate 603
TEA CUP. D 4⁵/₁₆in (109mm) Ht 2¹/₁₆in (52mm).
H. & R. Daniel, pattern number 6289, cup of Daniel's Second Bell shape with scalloped edge decorated with a dark blue ground, enamelled flower sprays and raised gilding, D handle with two spurs. *The Berthoud Collection.*

Plate 604
COFFEE CUP. D 3¾in (95mm) Ht 2⅞in (72mm).
H. & R. Daniel, pattern number 6112, cup of Daniel's First Bell shape, similar to that shown in Plate 603 but with a moulded border and the interior faceted, decorated with yellow scrolls and leaves on a maroon ground and with enamelled flowers, D handle with two spurs. *The Berthoud Collection.*

Plate 605
TEA CUP. D 4in (101mm) Ht 2⅜in (60mm).
Alcock, pattern number 8016, cup with moulded rim, decorated with a buff ground and enamelled flower spray D handle with a single spur pointing towards the cup. *Dr. Geoffrey & Alma Barnes Collection.*

Plate 606
COFFEE CUP. D 3¼in (82mm) Ht 2½in (63mm).
Factory unknown, pattern number 233, twelve sided cup on six moulded feet, decorated with a band of yellow, maroon dots and gilding and a flower spray in the centre, complex moulded handle. *Private Collection.*

Plate 607
TEA CUP. D 3⁵⁄₁₆in (84mm) Ht 1⅜in (35mm).
Factory unknown, no mark, slightly shanked cup (compare Plates 455 and 456) with moulded loop handle (compare Plates 611 and 617) decorated inside with a blue and orange floral pattern. *Private Collection.*

Plate 608
TEA CUP. D 3¾in (95mm) Ht 2¼in (56mm).
Davenport, brown wreath mark and pattern number 730, of porringer shape with a flared lip, decorated inside with single roses and gilt leaves. *City Museum & Art Gallery, Stoke-on-Trent.*

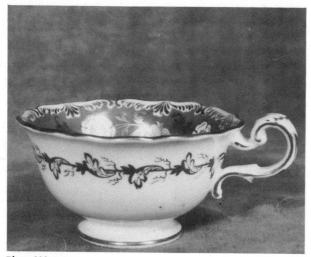

Plate 609
TEA CUP. D 4⅛in (104mm) Ht 2⅛in (53mm).
Coalport, pattern number 2/563, scalloped and moulded edge cup with feathered handle, decorated inside with elaborate green and yellow grounds, central enamelled flowers and rich gilding. *The Berthoud Collection.*

Plate 610
TEA CUP. D 4³⁄₁₆in (106mm) Ht 2in (50mm).
Coalport, pattern number 2/641, scallop and moulded edge cup decorated with enamelled flowers and trailing gilt 'fibre'. Wares in this shape with the moulding picked out in green have been recorded bearing the anomalous pattern number E/60. *Private Collection.*

Plate 611
COFFEE CUP. D 3³⁄₁₆in (81mm) Ht 2¹¹⁄₁₆in (68mm).
Coalport, no mark, cup with moulded rim on a pedestal base, decorated with a green seaweed pattern. *The Berthoud Collection.*

Plate 612
COFFEE CUP. D 3½in (89mm) Ht 2¾in (69mm).
Coalport, pattern number 4/647, moulded edge cup with leaf motif inside, the handle with moulded leaf thumb rest and divided upper attachment. Decorated with blue and buff leaves and gilt acorns. *The Berthoud Collection.*

Plate 613
TEA CUP. D 3⅞in (98mm) Ht 2in (50mm).
Ridgway, pattern number 2/2748, beautifully potted cup with flared lip, decorated with green and yellow leaves and sprays of enamel flowers, elaborate gilding, high loop handle. *Dr. Geoffrey & Alma Barnes Collection.*

Plate 614
TEA CUP. D 3in (76mm) Ht 2½in (63mm).
Probably Ridgway, no mark, cup with slightly scalloped edge decorated with a gilt border inside and enamelled flowers inside and out, handle of similar form to that shown in Plate 613. *Private Collection.*

Plate 615
COFFEE CUP. D 3¼in (82mm) Ht 2⁷⁄₁₆in (61mm).
Ridgway, pattern number 2/2054, cup with four pairs of spiral flutes on the upper part, pedestal base, high scrolling handle, decorated with enamelled flowers reserved in a band of grey. *Private Collection.*

Plate 616
COFFEE CUP. D 3in (76mm) Ht 2½in (63mm).
Factory unknown, no mark, decorated with gilt lines outside and a border of pink bell flowers inside, tightly coiled handle. Possibly New Hall. *Philip Miller.*

Plate 617
TEA CUP. D 4⅛in (104mm) Ht 2½in (63mm).
Ridgway, pattern 2/5758, cup with flared lip decorated with a grey ground and gilding (see Godden (16) Plate 91). *Private Collection.*

Plate 618
TEA CUP. D 4in (101mm) Ht 2⅛in (53mm).
Probably Ridgway, no mark, cup of similar form to that shown in Plate 617 except for a gentle curve towards the base, decorated with a blue ground, white panels with yellow borders, rather fussy gilding. *Private Collection.*

Plate 619
TEA CUP. D 3⅞in (98mm) Ht 1⅞in (48mm).
Paris, no mark, the cup that clearly inspired the French shape at Minton's and elsewhere (not to be confused with the earlier shape also called French, Plates 247-258), decorated inside with a pink ground and gilt lines, concave sides and tight loop handle. *Christopher May.*

Plate 620
TEA CUP. D 3¹⁵⁄₁₆in (100mm) Ht 2in (50mm).
Minton, pattern number 829, finely potted in a clear white body with loop handle, shown in the Minton shape book as 'B, French Shape', decorated with a yellow ground and puce lines. *The Berthoud Collection.*

Plate 621
COFFEE CUP. D 3⅛in (79mm) Ht 2½in (63mm).
Minton, pattern number 724, finely potted in a clear white body with loop handle, 'B, French Shape' in the Minton shape book, decorated with a yellow band inside and enamel flowers. Patterns in the range 700 to 1100 may be found. *The Berthoud Collection.*

Plate 622
COFFEE CUP. D 3⅛in (79mm) Ht 2⅜in (60mm).
Minton, pattern number 837, of similar form to 'B' but with a moulded rim and handle and moulded vine leaf base above four feet. Shown as 'G, Berlin Embossed' in the Minton shape book, decorated with enamelled flowers. Patterns in the range 830-1130 may be found. *The Berthoud Collection.*

Plate 623
TEA CUP. D 3⅞in (72mm) Ht 2in (50mm).
Hilditch, marked 'Q', cup of French shape decorated with lilac sprigging in abstract scrolls, loop handle similar to Minton's (Helm (21) Shape C3). *Private Collection.*

Plate 624
TEA CUP. D 3³⁄₁₆in (97mm) Ht 2¹⁄₁₆in (52mm).
Hilditch, no mark, cup of French shape (Helm (21) Shape C3) decorated with an orange print embellished with green and blue enamels. *Philip Miller.*

Plate 625
COFFEE CUP. D 3⅜in (86mm) Ht 2½in (63mm).
Minton, pattern number 3182, a scalloped edge cup with loop handle rising above the rim, decorated inside with a dark blue ground, enamelled flowers and gilding. This shape does not appear in the Minton shape book. *Jean Sewell Antiques.*

Plate 626
COFFEE CUP. D 3⁵⁄₁₆in (84mm) Ht 2¹³⁄₁₆in (71mm).
Factory unknown, no mark, cup with flared lip and very large loop handle divided at the top, decorated inside with blue and buff panels in a four arched pattern with enamelled flowers. *Philip Miller.*

Plate 627
TEA CUP. D 4⅛in (104mm) Ht 2⅛in (53mm).
Probably Alcock, no marks, decorated inside with a maroon ground, thin stemmed flowers in panels bordered in yellow, high quality gilding, moulded loop handle touching the rim of the cup with very wide upper attachment. *The Berthoud Collection.*

Plate 628
COFFEE CUP. D 3³⁄₁₆in (81mm) Ht 2½in (63mm).
Probably Alcock, pattern 2719 (on matching square dishes with corner handles), decorated inside with a green ground, reserved white ribbons and panels and enamelled birds nests with eggs, moulded loop handle touching the rim of the cup. *The Berthoud Collection.*

Plate 629
TEA CUP. D 3⅞in (98mm) Ht 2³⁄₁₆in (55mm).
Factory unknown, no marks, cup of similar shape to that shown in Plate 627 but with inner moulded border, less flared lip and loop handle standing high and clear of the rim, decorated inside with a green ground, gilt border and enamelled flower sprays. *The Berthoud Collection.*

Plate 630
COFFEE CUP. D 3³⁄₁₆in (81mm) Ht 2⅜in (60mm).
Factory unknown, no marks, cup of similar form to that shown in Plate 629 with moulded inner border, decorated with an orange and blue Imari pattern, moulded loop handle standing clear of the rim. *City Museum & Art Gallery, Stoke-on-Trent.*

Plate 631
TEA CUP. D 3¹³/₁₆in (97mm) Ht 2in (50mm).
Rockingham, pattern number 2/4, the saucer marked with a puce griffin and 'Rockingham Works, Brameld, Manufacturer to the King', basket weave moulding with knobbed rustic handle, decorated with gilding only. *The Berthoud Collection.*

Plate 632
TEA CUP. D 3⅝in (92mm) Ht 2¹/₁₆in (52mm).
Rockingham, no marks, fluted cup of similar form to that shown in Plate 631 with knobbed rustic handle, decorated with blue sprigging in the form of shells alternating with paterae (Plate 672 shows the same shell sprigging inverted). *Bruce Newmane.*

Plate 633
LARGE TEA CUP. D 3¾in (95mm) Ht 2⅛in (53mm).
Coalport, pattern number 2/310, fluted cup with a narrow panel alternating with two broad panels, kicked loop handle, decorated with a blue printed pattern of prunus blossom and spiky winged butterflies picked out in gold (compare Plate 542). This pattern may also occur in pink or brown. *Jean Sewell Antiques.*

Plate 634
TEA CUP. D 3⅝in (92mm) Ht 2³/₁₆in (55mm).
Coalport, impressed numeral 5 on the saucer, fluted cup decorated with a flower pattern in coloured enamels over a black printed outline, brown on the rim and loop handle. *Clive House Museum, Shrewsbury.*

Plate 635
TEA CUP. D 3⅝in (92mm) Ht 2in (50mm).
Attributed to Grainger, pattern number 18 on the saucer, osier moulded border (compare rather finer example in Plate 263), decorated with enamelled flowers inside and out, loop handle. *D.R. Pomfret.*

Plate 636
TEA CUP. D 3¾in (69mm) Ht 2¼in (56mm).
Grainger, marked 'Grainger & Co., Worcester', scallop edged cup decorated inside and out with a blue printed dragon design, kicked loop handle. *The Dyson Perrins Museum, Worcester.*

Plate 637
TEA CUP. D 3½in (89mm) Ht 2¼in (56mm).
Minton, pattern number B571+ and impressed 'Minton's' on the saucer (post 1871), shallow Bute shape cup decorated with printed and enamelled flowers, loop handle. *Liz Jackson Antiques.*

Plate 638
TEA CUP. D 3¾in (95mm) Ht 2⅛in (53mm).
Probably Minton, no mark, rim with four broad and four narrow lobes alternating, decorated with three printed shells inside and out, loop handle with rudimentary inner spur. *Doremy Antiques, Herne Bay.*

Plate 639
TEA CUP. D 3⅝in (92mm) Ht 2in (50mm).
Factory unknown, pattern number 4/3829, fluted cup with two broad panels alternating with one narrow, decorated inside with a yellow ground, panels of enamel flowers, peasant figures in the centre and elaborate gilding, loop handle with outer spur. *E.G. Stevenson.*

Plate 640
TEA CUP. L 3⅝in (92mm) Ht 2in (50mm).
Factory unknown, no mark, shallow fluted cup with two broad panels alternating with one narrow, decorated with pink roses and finely drawn purple leaves, loop handle with outer spur. *Private Collection.*

Plate 641
TEA CUP. D 3¹³/₁₆in (97mm) Ht 2in (50mm).
Factory unknown, no marks, shallow cup decorated inside and out with a blue floral printed pattern, loop handle with outer spur. *Liz Jackson Antiques.*

Plate 642
TEA CUP. D 3⅝in (92mm) Ht 2⅛in (53mm).
Probably Hilditch, no mark, shallow cup decorated with an orange print of a Chinaman carrying two birds on a perch, embellished with blue and green enamels, loop handle with outer spur. *The Berthoud Collection.*

Plate 643
TEA CUP. D 3¹¹⁄₁₆in (94mm) Ht 1¹⁵⁄₁₆in (49mm).
Chamberlain, pattern number 1030, scallop edged cup with distinctive handle decorated with a dark blue ground, enamelled flowers and gilding. (see Plate 576). *The Dyson Perrins Museum, Worcester.*

Plate 644
COFFEE CUP. D 3³⁄₁₆in (81mm) Ht 2½in (63mm).
Chamberlain, from a service with plates impressed 'CHAMBERLAIN'S WORCESTER', pattern number 1030, heavy cup in a glassy body with distinctive handle, decorated with a dark blue ground and enamelled flowers (see Plate 576). *The Berthoud Collection.*

Plate 645
TEA CUP. D 3¾in (95mm) Ht 2⅛in (53mm).
Hilditch, no mark but conforming to pattern 44, scallop edged cup, the upright to the handle curving away from the cup at the top. Decorated with barbeaux sprays inside and out. *Dover Street Antiques, Canterbury.*

Plate 646
COFFEE CUP. D 3¼in (82mm) Ht 2⅝in (66mm).
Chamberlain, pattern number 1399, cup of so-called 'Octagon' (twelve sided) shape in a thick smooth glassy body, decorated with a band of blue sprays inside with single flowers in reserved panels. *The Berthoud Collection.*

Plate 647
TEA CUP. D 3¼in (82mm) Ht 2¼in (56mm).
Ridgway, pattern number 2/831, cup with flared rim with embossed trellis moulding and moulded asymmetrical cartouches decorated with green vine leaves and gilding. A similar form also occurs without the moulding. *The Berthoud Collection.*

Plate 648
TEA CUP. D 3½in (89mm) Ht 2⁵⁄₁₆in (58mm).
C.J. Mason, no mark, finely moulded cup with basket weave and cartouches decorated with an enamelled Chinese scene inside and out (see Godden (10) Plates 203-205). *Warner Antiques, Brasted, Kent.*

Plate 649
TEA CUP. D 3⅛in (79mm) Ht 2⅛in (53mm).
Factory unknown, no mark, moulded leaf border which has been likened to melting snow on a roof, decorated with enamelled flowers and gilding, curiously moulded handle. Patterns in the range 1674-2003 may be found on the tea wares. *The Berthoud Collection.*

Plate 650
COFFEE CUP. D 2¹⁵⁄₁₆in (74mm) Ht 2½in (63mm).
Factory unknown, pattern number 1674, moulded 'Melting Snow' border, decorated inside with a dark blue ground, enamelled flowers and elaborate gilding. A wide variety of decorative styles may be found on these cups. *The Berthoud Collection.*

Plate 651
TEA CUP. D 3⅝in (92mm) Ht 2¹⁄₁₆in (52mm).
Factory unknown, pattern number 1565, cup with moulded rim and base, decorated with a pale yellow band inside with enamelled shells and gilding, handle with inner spur and with the top usually gilded. *Dr. Geoffrey & Alma Barnes Collection.*

Plate 652
COFFEE CUP. D 3³⁄₁₆in (81mm) Ht 2½in (63mm).
Factory unknown, pattern number 1213, cup with moulded rim and base, decorated with a dark blue ground, reserved groups of white flowers and gilding. A wide variety of patterns may be found in the range 1100-1565. *M. Jacobs Antiques, Tenterden, Kent.*

Plate 653
TEA CUP. D 4in (101mm) Ht 2in (50mm).
Factory unknown, pattern number 1710, cup of plain shape on a pedestal base, decorated with an apricot ground with white reserved leaves and rather clumsy gilding, convoluted handle similar to a Paris shape. *The Berthoud Collection.*

Plate 654
COFFEE CUP. D 3in (76mm) Ht 2¾in (69mm).
Factory unknown, pattern number 1717 in gold, decorated with a broad green band inside with pink shells and acanthus leaves and scrolls surrounding cartouches containing enamelled flowers, complex Paris type handle. *The Berthoud Collection.*

Plate 655
TEA CUP. D 3¾in (95mm) Ht 2³⁄₁₆in (55mm).
Ridgway, no mark, waisted pedestal cup with scalloped rim and a row of moulded florets round the base, decorated with a brown and yellow floral printed pattern, (see Godden (16) Plate 88). *The Berthoud Collection.*

Plate 656
COFFEE CUP. D 3⁵⁄₁₆in (84mm) Ht 2¾in (69mm).
Ridgway, pattern number 2/3510, cup of similar shape to that shown in Plate 655, decorated with large green enamel moths and gilt leaves, a row of moulded florets round the base. *The Berthoud Collection.*

Plate 657
TEA CUP. D 3¾in (95mm) Ht 2¼in (56mm).
William Ridgway, no mark, waisted earthenware cup of bluish-mauve body glazed and decorated with enamelled flowers in a typical palette of similar shape to those shown in Plates 655 and 656 but with thinner handle and spur and no moulded florets. *Philip Miller.*

Plate 658
TEA CUP. D 3¾in (95mm) Ht 2⅜in (60mm).
Factory unknown, pattern number 853, moulded cup decorated with a buff ground and gilt stems, handle formed of opposing scrolls. *Christopher May.*

Plate 659
TEA CUP. D 3⅞in (98mm) Ht 2¼in (56mm).
Ridgway, pattern number 2/4050, waisted cup with pedestal foot, slightly scalloped edge decorated with a bright apricot ground, white flowers and leaves and gilt leaves and scrolls, well modelled handle. *The Berthoud Collection.*

Plate 660
TEA CUP. D 3¹³⁄₁₆in (97mm) Ht 2½in (63mm).
Factory unknown, pattern number 1376, ribbed cup decorated inside with a pattern of gilt pendant bells, handle of similar form to that shown in Plate 659 but less well modelled. *Christopher May.*

Plate 661
TEA CUP. D 3¾in (95mm) Ht 2¹/₁₆in (52mm).
Hilditch, pattern 413, ribbed and scalloped edge cup, decorated inside with a bright green ground, yellow panels and gilding, handle with top spur (Helm (21) Shape B4). *The Berthoud Collection.*

Plate 662
TEA CUP. D 3⁹/₁₆in (90mm) Ht 2⅜in (60mm).
Hilditch, no mark, plain edge cup decorated with a grey foxglove print picked out in gold, smaller handle than that shown in Plate 661. *Bill Dickenson, Ironbridge.*

Plate 663
TEA CUP. D 3¾in (95mm) Ht 2⅜in (60mm).
Hilditch, no mark, plain unmoulded cup decorated with a black printed 'Sheltering Peasants' pattern (see Halfpenny and Lockett (11) Plate 122), handle with top spur (Helm (21) Shape B4). *The Berthoud Collection.*

Plate 664
TEA CUP. D 3¾in (95mm) Ht 2³/₁₆in (55mm).
Probably Hilditch, no mark, earthenware cup of similar shape to that shown in Plate 663 but with lower handle and smaller spur, decorated inside and out with a purple print of peasants harvesting. *The Berthoud Collection.*

Plate 665
TEA CUP. D 3⅞in (98mm) Ht 2¼in (56mm).
Hilditch and Sons c. 1830, pattern number 407 in pink lustre, bone china cup with fluted moulding ending below a flared, scalloped lip, decorated with lilac sprigging inside and out and with a pink rose with green leaves in the centre (see Halfpenny and Lockett (11) Plate 127). *Private Collection.*

Plate 666
TEA CUP. D 3¾in (95mm) Ht 2in (50mm).
Factory unknown, pattern number 1262, plain edge cup decorated inside and out with lilac sprigging, lower handle form, possibly Hilditch. *Philip Miller.*

Plate 667
TEA CUP. D 4¹/₁₆in (103mm) Ht 2in (50mm).
Hilditch, pattern number 444, moulded edge cup with thickly potted handle having two outer and one inner spur, decorated with a green plaid pattern, gilding and a central flower spray (Helm (21) Shape A5). *The Berthoud Collection.*

Plate 668
TEA CUP. D 4in (101mm) Ht 2¹/₁₆in (52mm).
Factory unknown, no mark, cup with moulded border, decorated with three flower sprays and gilt initials AH, three spur handle similar to that of Hilditch (Plate 667) but thinner and meaner. *D.R. Pomfret.*

Plate 669
TEA CUP. D 4¹/₁₆in (103mm) Ht 2in (50mm).
Rockingham, pattern number 1453, four lobed cup decorated with grey leaves and gilding, the delicately modelled handle with three spurs. *The Berthoud Collection.*

Plate 670
COFFEE CUP. D 3½in (89mm) Ht 2¹¹/₁₆in (68mm).
Rockingham, pattern number 1212, four lobed cup decorated with a grey leaf pattern and some gilding, typical three spur handle. *The Berthoud Collection.*

Plate 671
TEA CUP. D 4in (101mm) Ht 2¹/₁₆in (52mm).
Rockingham, no mark, moulded edge cup decorated with a grey ground and gilt fibre pattern, handle with single spur (see Rice (18) Plates 113 and 114). *The Berthoud Collection.*

Plate 672
COFFEE CUP. D 3⁵/₁₆in (84mm) Ht 2¹³/₁₆in (71mm).
Rockingham, pattern number 891 on the saucer, plain shape cup with blue sprigging in the form of shells (compare Plate 632), the rustic single spur handle is extremely rare. *Bruce Newmane.*

Plate 673
TEA CUP. D 2⅞in (72mm) Ht 1¹¹⁄₁₆in (43mm).
Rockingham, pattern number 1290 and puce griffin mark on the saucer, miniature cup with large loop handle, not of recognized Rockingham shape, decorated with a green ground and seaweed gilding. *Bruce Newmane*

Plate 674
COFFEE CAN. D 2¹⁵⁄₁₆in (74mm) Ht 2¾in (69mm).
Rockingham, celebration coffee can, pattern number 826 in gold and Royal Rockingham mark on the saucer, decorated with enamelled flowers and gilding, horse's hoof handle (see also Plates 430 and 431). *Bruce Newmane.*

Plate 675
COFFEE CUP. D 3½in (89mm) Ht 2¾in (69mm).
Hilditch, pattern number 2068, cup of plain shape with flared lip and pedestal foot, decorated inside with a dark blue ground and gilt grapes, enamelled rose in the centre, plain loop handle (Helm (21) Shape A3). *D.R. Pomfret.*

Plate 676
TEA CUP. D 3¼in (82mm) Ht 3⅝in (92mm).
Factory unknown, pattern number 2421, cup with a band of short moulded ribs, decorated with a fawn ground, gilding and enamelled flowers, moulded rope handle with small outer spur (see Plate 510). *Jean Sewell Antiques.*

Plate 677
TEA CUP. D 3⁷⁄₁₆in (87mm) Ht 2½in (63mm).
Hilditch and Hopwood, pattern number 2516, cup with slightly scalloped edge decorated with a fawn ground and gilding and with a flower spray in the centre, loop handle with upper and lower spur (Helm (21) Shape A2). *Private Collection.*

Plate 678
COFFEE CUP. D 3in (76mm) Ht 2¹³⁄₁₆in (71mm).
Hilditch & Hopwood, no mark, plain edged cup with pedestal foot decorated with an elaborate pattern inside and out, handle similar to that in Plate 677 with upper and lower spurs (Helm (21) Shape A2). *Private Collection.*

Plate 679
TEA CUP. D 3¹⁵⁄₁₆in (100mm) Ht 2in (50mm).
Minton, pattern number 2390, cup with slightly scalloped rim and two finely embossed floral panels, decorated with a rich blue ground and enamelled flowers, the handle with horizontal thumb rest and inner spur, designated 'L, Clarendon' in the Minton shape book. *Patricia Ratcliffe Antiques.*

Plate 680
COFFEE CUP. D 3³⁄₁₆in (81mm) Ht 2⅝in (66mm).
Minton, pattern number 2390, coffee cup matching that shown in Plate 679, this rather rare shape is designated 'L, Clarendon' in the Minton shape book, loop handle with two spurs, the lower inside. *Patricia Ratcliffe Antiques.*

Plate 681
TEA CUP. D 4⅛in (104mm) Ht 2¼in (56mm).
Derby, Bloor period crown and Gothic D mark, cup with flared lip and pedestal foot, decorated inside with a blue border, enamelled flowers and gilt grapes and leaves, loop handle with two spurs (compare Plate 679). *Bill Dickenson, Ironbridge.*

Plate 682
COFFEE CUP. D 3⁹⁄₁₆in (90mm) Ht 2⅝in (66mm).
Derby, Bloor period crown and Gothic D mark, coffee cup matching that shown in Plate 681 with two spur handle. *Private Collection.*

Plate 683
BREAKFAST CUP. D 4¼in (107mm) Ht 2⁷⁄₁₆in (61mm).
Derby, Bloor Derby circle mark, flattened Bute shape decorated with a green border and gilding, horizontal thumb rest and inner spur (compare Plates 679 and 681). *The Berthoud Collection.*

Plate 684
TEA CUP. D 3¼in (82mm) Ht 1¾in (69mm).
Davenport, marked Davenport in underglaze blue with pattern name 'Casino' and number 715, of porringer shape with loop handle with thumb rest, decorated inside and out with an underglaze blue pattern with on-glaze orange flowers. *Stable Antiques, Wingham, Kent.*

Plate 685
COFFEE CUP. D 3⅛in (79mm) Ht 2⅜in (60mm).
Factory unknown, pattern 314, cup with seven moulded spiral flutes, decorated inside with a dark blue ground with yellow panels and elaborate gilding, from the same factory as the cup shown in Plates 567, 568 and 691. *The Berthoud Collection.*

Plate 686
COFFEE CUP. D 3⅜in (86mm) Ht 2⅝in (66mm).
Davenport, puce crown mark and 'Davenport, Longport, Staffordshire', bell shaped cup with uncharacteristic handle decorated with printed and enamelled flowers and a gilt inner border. *Private Collection.*

Plate 687
TEA CUP. D 4⅛in (104mm) Ht 2in (50mm).
Factory unknown, pattern number 175/7, shallow cup decorated inside with a dark blue ground, enamel flowers and elaborate gilding, small handle with vertical spur. *Jean Sewell Antiques.*

Plate 688
COFFEE CUP. D 3⁵⁄₁₆in (84mm) Ht 2⅝in (66mm).
Factory unknown, no mark, coffee cup of a shape matching that shown in Plate 687, decorated with a band of pale yellow with enamelled flowers, small handle with vertical spur. *The Berthoud Collection.*

Plate 689
TEA CUP. D 3½in (89mm) Ht 2in (50mm).
Dixon Phillips & Co. (Sunderland), impressed mark, earthenware cup decorated with lustre and green enamel. *Philip Miller.*

Plate 690
TEA CUP. D 3¹³⁄₁₆in (97mm) Ht 2in (50mm).
Machin & Potts, printed Staffordshire knot mark and 'Machin & Potts, Printed, Staffordshire Potteries' and pattern number 1263, shallow cup decorated with a blue printed pattern inside and out with gilt embellishment, well formed handle. *Dr. Geoffrey & Alma Barnes Collection.*

Plate 691
TEA CUP. D 3¼in (82mm) Ht 2¼in (56mm).
Factory unknown, pattern number 250, cup of the same basic shape as that shown in Plate 567 but lacking the border moulding and with more restrained handle, decorated with a buff ground and gilding. *The Berthoud Collection.*

Plate 692
COFFEE CUP. D 3¼in (82mm) Ht 2⅝in (66mm).
Factory unknown, pattern number 1880, twelve sided cup decorated with a green ground in panels, gilt anthemion and spray, moulded handle with thumb rest. A similar cup of pattern number 1819 is back stamped in orange 'Yates, Leeds' (probably a retailer's mark on a Herculaneum cup). *The Berthoud Collection.*

Plate 693
TEA CUP. D 3⅞in (98mm) Ht 2⅛in (53mm).
Spode, pattern number 4738 and H, Spode's '4643' shape (see Whiter (7) page 129) with wavy edge and flat top handle, decorated with a blue ground and gilding. *The Berthoud Collection.*

Plate 694
COFFEE CUP. D 3⅞in (98mm) Ht 3in (76mm).
Copeland & Garrett, 'Late Spode's' felspar back stamp and pattern number 4710, decorated inside with triple flowers with raised gilding and heavy dark green leaves, c. 1833. *The Berthoud Collection.*

Plate 695
TEA CUP. D 3⅝in (92mm) Ht 1⅞in (48mm).
Factory A, pattern number 1612, six lobed cup of similar shape to Spode's 4643 shape (Plate 693) with smaller handle and less well formed spur, decorated with a blue band and gilding. *The Berthoud Collection.*

Plate 696
TEA CUP. D 3¾in (95mm) Ht 1¹⁵⁄₁₆in (49mm).
Factory A, pattern number 1544, six lobed cup very similar in shape to both Spode 4643 shape (Plate 693 and compare Plate 694) but with the handle set at a steeper angle and with slightly feathered top, decorated with a green ground and gilding. *Philip Miller.*

Plate 697
COFFEE CUP. D 3in (76mm) Ht 2½in (63mm).
Copeland & Garrett, brown back stamp 'Copeland & Garrett late Spode', Spode's '5146' shape (see Whiter (7) page 130) introduced c. 1833 just before the change to Copeland & Garrett, melon shaped cup decorated with a fawn ground and gilding, the handle formed of two scrolls with a top spur (compare Plate 805). *City Museum & Art Gallery, Stoke-on-Trent.*

Plate 698
TEA CUP. D 3¾in (95mm) Ht 2¼in (56mm).
Factory unknown, pattern number 177, cup of basic London shape with flared lip, handle of similar form to Spode's 5146 shape but with outward pointing spur, decorated inside with orange and blue flowers and green leaves. *Gus Brain Antiques.*

Plate 699
TEA CUP. D 3⅜in (86mm) Ht 2¼in (56mm).
Davenport, marked 'Davenport, Longport' in blue, unusual melon shaped cup similar to Spode's 5146 shape (Plate 697) decorated with a blue and gold border and gilt thistles. *Private Collection.*

Plate 700
TEA CUP. D 3⅜in (86mm) Ht 2⅜in (60mm).
Factory unknown, no mark, melon shaped cup decorated with an Imari pattern in blue and orange, the handle similar to Davenport's (Plate 699) but with longer upper scroll. *Bill Dickenson, Ironbridge.*

Plate 701
COFFEE CUP, D 3¼in (82mm) Ht 2½in (63mm).
Minton, pattern number 1394B with embossed rococo swirls inside the cup and with feathered handle, designated 'F, Essex Embossed' in the Minton shape book, decorated with a dark blue ground and gilding. *Jean Sewell Antiques.*

Plate 702
TEA CUP. D 3⅞in (98mm) Ht 2¼in (56mm).
Minton, pattern number 1347, slightly scalloped edged cup with swirling internal moulding and with feathered handle, designated 'F, Essex Embossed' in the Minton shape book, decorated with an apricot band inside and delicate gilding. Another version also occurs with external moulded scrolls. *Dover Street Antiques, Canterbury, Kent.*

Plate 703
TEA CUP. D 3³⁄₁₆in (81mm) Ht 2in (50mm).
Minton, pattern number 1557, with wavy lip, embossed scrolls forming a cartouche and kicked loop handle, decorated with a dark blue ground, enamelled flowers and good gilding. This shape is designated 'C, Bath Embossed' in the Minton shape book. *The Berthoud Collection.*

Plate 704
COFFEE CUP. D 2³⁄₄in (69mm) Ht 2⁷⁄₁₆in (61mm).
Minton, printed back stamp 'Felspar China, no 41', a simpler version of Bath Embossed shape decorated with small blue printed flower sprays, with standard moulding for this shape but with smaller and less well formed handle (compare Plate 703). *The Berthoud Collection.*

Plate 705
TEA CUP. D 3⁷⁄₈in (98mm) Ht 2in (50mm).
Factory A, pattern number 1960, six lobed cup with moulded edge and large handle with feathered top, decorated inside with a blue ground and pink dog roses and an enamelled shell, this shape is closely linked with that shown in Plate 695. *The Berthoud Collection.*

Plate 706
COFFEE CUP. D 2⁹⁄₁₆in (64mm) Ht 2⁹⁄₁₆in (64mm).
Minton, pattern number N9560, a slightly fluted cup with well formed handle, decorated with a turquoise border and enamelled flowers. This shape does not appear in the Minton shape book. *City Museum & Art Gallery, Stoke-on-Trent.*

Plate 707
TEA CUP. D 3⁹⁄₁₆in (90mm) Ht 2⁷⁄₁₆in (61mm).
Factory A, pattern number 2094, shallow cup with plain edge, the handle being a simpler version of that shown in Plate 705, decorated inside with a dark blue ground and enamelled flowers and a fence, elaborately gilded. *Dr. Geoffrey & Alma Barnes Collection.*

Plate 708
TEA CUP. D 3⁷⁄₈in (98mm) Ht 2¹⁄₁₆in (52mm).
Factory unknown, no mark, moulded cup similar in form to that shown in Plate 705 but much blander, decorated with barbeaux sprig decoration in pink, blue and gold. *The Berthoud Collection.*

Plate 709
COFFEE CUP. D 3⅛in (79mm) Ht 2¾in (69mm).
Copeland & Garrett, felspar back stamp in green and pattern number 5370. Possibly the first new shape introduced by Copeland & Garrett, on thick moulded feet with moulded leaves and scrolls and complex handle, the mouldings picked out in gold on a cream ground with enamelled roses and butterflies. *The Berthoud Collection.*

Plate 710
COFFEE CUP. D 3⅛in (79mm) Ht 2⁹∕₁₆in (64mm).
Copeland & Garrett, crown mark in green and pattern number 6297, c. 1839, decorated with enamelled flowers and ribbons on a cream ground. *The Berthoud Collection.*

Plate 711
TEA CUP. D 3¾in (95mm) Ht 2⅜in (60mm).
Copeland & Garrett, crown and wreath mark, 'Berlin' in Gothic lettering and pattern number 6957, moulded cup on a high pedestal base decorated with a yellow ground, the mouldings picked out in blue with enamelled flowers, the handle in similar form to that shown in Plate 710. *Alan Townsend Collection.*

Plate 712
COFFEE CUP. D 3¹∕₁₆in (78mm) Ht 3¹∕₁₆in (78mm).
Copeland & Garrett, crown and wreath mark, 'Berlin' in Gothic lettering and pattern number 6884, coffee cup apparently matching the tea cup shown in Plate 711 but with a different pattern number and with slight differences in the palette employed. *Alan Townsend Collection.*

Plate 713
TEA CUP. D 3⅝in (92mm) Ht 2¾in (69mm).
Factory unknown, pattern number 2/40, slightly waisted cup decorated with an enamelled landscape and elaborate gilding, handle in the form of two scrolls with small upper spur. *Christopher May Antiques.*

Plate 714
COFFEE CUP. D 3¹⁵∕₁₆in (100mm) Ht 2⅞in (72mm).
Factory unknown, pattern number 2/40, only slightly narrower coffee cup matching the tea cup shown in Plate 713. *Christopher May Antiques.*

Plate 715
TEA CUP. D 3¹¹⁄₁₆in (94mm) Ht 2¼in (56mm).
C.J. Mason, no mark, ironstone cup with flared lip, decorated with an Imari pattern, heavy loop handle. *The Haggar Collection, City Museum & Art Gallery, Stoke-on-Trent.*

Plate 716
COFFEE CUP. D 3⅜in (86mm) Ht 2⅝in (66mm).
C.J.Mason, no mark, coffee cup matching the tea cup shown in Plate 715, with additional embellishment to the handle. *The Haggar Collection, City Museum & Art Gallery, Stoke-on-Trent.*

Plate 717
TEA CUP. D 3¹¹⁄₁₆in (94mm) Ht 2⅛in (53mm).
C.J. Mason, no mark, ironstone cup with flared lip, decorated inside with a dark blue ground with gilt holly leaves and a rose in the centre, gilded handle rather smaller than that shown in Plates 715 and 716. *Christopher May.*

Plate 718
COFFEE CUP. D 3³⁄₁₆in (81mm) Ht 2⅝in (66mm).
C.J. Mason, standard printed mark, twelve sided heavily modelled ironstone cup of very uneven shape, decorated with a typical Imari pattern, heavily modelled handle in the form of a serpent (see Godden (10) Plate 248). *Christopher May.*

Plate 719
TEA CUP. D 3⅞in (98mm) Ht 2in (50mm).
C.J. Mason, no mark, bone china cup with eight broad and eight narrow facets, decorated with a printed Japan pattern over painted in enamel colours, high handle with a top spur. *D.R. Pomfret.*

Plate 720
COFFEE CUP. D 3³⁄₁₆in (81mm) Ht 2⁹⁄₁₆in (64mm).
C.J. Mason, no mark, cup matching that shown in Plate 719. *D.R. Pomfret.*

Plate 721
TEA CUP. D 4in (101mm) Ht 3½in (89mm).
C.J.Mason, pattern number 315, twelve faceted bone china cup decorated with a green ground and black panels in underglaze colours, unusual handle form. *Jean Sewell Antiques.*

Plate 722
COFFEE CUP. D 3½in (89mm) Ht 2⅜in (60mm).
C.J. Mason, pattern number 315, coffee cup matching that shown in Plate 721 but with a completely different handle form with a large ring and top spur. *Jean Sewell Antiques.*

Plate 723
TEA CUP. D 3⅞in (98mm) Ht 2in (50mm).
C.J.Mason, no mark, scallop edged bone china cup decorated with a printed and enamelled pattern, high oval ring handle with a vertical spur. *Bill Dickenson, Ironbridge.*

Plate 724
COFFEE CUP. D 3⁷⁄₁₆in (87mm) Ht 2⁹⁄₁₆in (64mm).
C.J. Mason, no mark, cup matching that shown in Plate 723. *Bill Dickenson, Ironbridge.*

Plate 725
TEA CUP. D 3⅞in (98mm) Ht 2in (50mm).
C.J.Mason, no mark, ribbed bone china cup with flared lip, decorated with a dull green ground with pale yellow and enamelled flowers, ring and spur handle (compare Plates 722, 723 and 724). *Jean Sewell Antiques.*

Plate 726
COFFEE CUP. D 3¹⁄₁₆in (78mm) Ht 2⁹⁄₁₆in (64mm).
C.J. Mason, wavy edged bone china cup decorated with a brown printed pattern embellished with coloured enamels, loop handle with rudimentary inner spur. *Bill Dickenson, Ironbridge.*

Plate 727
TEA CUP. D 3⅞in (98mm) H 2in (50mm).
C.J.Mason, printed mark, wavy edged cup decorated inside with an Imari pattern in enamel colours, loop handle with vertical spur. *The Haggar Collection, City Museum & Art Gallery, Stoke-on-Trent.*

Plate 728
COFFEE CUP. D 3⅛in (79mm) Ht 2³⁄₁₆in (55mm).
C.J.Mason, no mark, cup matching that shown in Plate 727 but with an additional spur pointing towards the cup. *The Haggar Collection, City Museum & Art Gallery, Stoke-on-Trent.*

Plate 729
TEA CUP. D 3⅞in (98mm) Ht 1¹⁵⁄₁₆in (49mm).
C.J.Mason, no mark, ribbed bone china cup with iron red, green and yellow pattern over a brown print, handle with high vertical spur and additional smaller spur. *The Berthoud Collection.*

Plate 730
COFFEE CUP. D 3in (76mm) Ht 2¼in (56mm).
C.J. Mason, ribbed bone china cup, decorated with a printed and enamelled pattern of flowers and butterflies. *The Berthoud Collection.*

Plate 731
COFFEE CUP. D 3⅛in (79mm) Ht 2½in (63mm).
C.J.Mason, bone china cup with flared and slightly scalloped lip, decorated with an ironstone type printed and enamelled pattern, the handle with two spurs. *Mona & Gerald Sattin.*

Plate 732
COFFEE CUP. D 3⁵⁄₁₆in (84mm) Ht 2⁷⁄₁₆in (61mm).
C.J. Mason, no mark, ribbed bone china cup decorated with a printed and enamelled pattern and gilding. *The Berthoud Collection.*

Plate 733
TEA CUP. D 3⁹⁄₁₆in (90mm) Ht 2⁵⁄₁₆in (58mm).
Enoch Wood, no mark, earthenware cup excavated from the foundations of St. Paul's Church, Burslem, decorated with a pinkish brown print of a girl with a bird on one side and a boy with a goat on the other, handle similar to that in Plate 734. *City Museum & Art Gallery, Stoke-on-Trent.*

Plate 734
TEA CUP. D 3⅝in (92mm) Ht 2¼in (56mm).
Hilditch & Son, crowned wreath and H&S mark, tea cup with flared lip, decorated in a thick inky blue with Chinese figures outside and reserved white flowers within, coiled handle with top spur (Helm (21) Shape C2), (compare Enoch Wood cup Plate 733). *The Berthoud Collection.*

Plate 735
TEA CUP. D 3¾in (95mm) Ht 2⅜in (60mm).
Enoch Wood, no mark, slightly translucent cup excavated from the foundations of St. Paul's Church, Burslem, decorated with a blue transfer printed floral pattern. *City Museum & Art Gallery, Stoke-on-Trent.*

Plate 736
TEA CUP. D 3¾in (95mm) Ht 2³⁄₁₆in (55mm).
Factory unknown, ribbed bone china cup with eight broad and eight narrow panels, decorated with a blue transfer printed floral pattern inside and out, complex handle. *The Berthoud Collection.*

Plate 737
TEA CUP. D 3⁹⁄₁₆in (90mm) Ht 2⅛in (53mm).
Factory unknown, pattern 76, scallop edged cup decorated with groups of three flowers in shades of purple and pink, handle with high spur, possibly Hilditch. *The Berthoud Collection.*

Plate 738
TEA CUP. D 3¹³⁄₁₆in (97mm) Ht 2⅛in (53mm).
Hilditch & Son, crowned H&S mark, scallop edged cup decorated with Chinese figures in pink and green enamels, handle with high spur (Helm (21) Shape C4). *Philip Miller.*

Plate 739
COFFEE CUP. D 3¼in (82mm) Ht 2¹¹⁄₁₆in (68mm).
G.F. Bowers, registered mark for 1848 and the saucer marked 'Lizard Pattern', very fine white bone china body, decorated with a blue bodied dragon with a pink head and leaves and gilt flowers, loop handle with upper and lower spurs. *The Berthoud Collection.*

Plate 740
COFFEE CUP. D 3¹⁄₁₆in (78mm) Ht 2¹¹⁄₁₆in (68mm).
Grainger, pattern number 1592, gadroon edged cup decorated inside with a dark green border with narrow gilt gadrooning, a convolvulus flower in the centre. *B & A Downes Antiques.*

Plate 741
TEA CUP. D 3⁹⁄₁₆in (90mm) Ht 2¼in (56mm).
Factory unknown, cup with slightly flared lip, covered with finely modelled scroll moulding and decorated with single roses and gilding, loop handle with two spurs (compare Plate 739). *Bill Dickenson, Ironbridge.*

Plate 742
COFFEE CUP. D 2⅝in (66mm) Ht 2⅜in (60mm).
Factory unknown, cup matching that shown in Plate 741. *Bill Dickenson, Ironbridge.*

Plate 743
TEA CUP. D 3½in (89mm) Ht 2½in (63mm).
Davenport, blue wreath mark and pattern number 2604, Bute shape with loop handle, decorated with an on-glaze printed with pink roses and green leaves. *The Berthoud Collection.*

Plate 744
COFFEE CUP. D 3in (76mm) Ht 2⁷⁄₁₆in (61mm).
Davenport, blue wreath mark, cup with moulded scrolls gilt and picked out in turquoise enamel. *City Museum & Art Gallery, Stoke-on-Trent.*

Plate 745
TEA CUP. D 3⁹⁄₁₆in (90mm) Ht 2⅛in (53mm).
Minton, pattern number N2532, shallow cup with kicked loop handle designated 'D, Regent Shape' in the Minton shape book, decorated with a combed blue edge with printed and enamelled flowers. *Christopher May.*

Plate 746
TEA CUP. D 3⅞in (98mm) Ht 2¹⁄₁₆in (52mm).
Ridgway, Royal Arms mark, and pattern number 2/6176, the saucer marked 'Madrigal', decorated with an Imari floral pattern in blue and orange, handle with more pronounced kick than on the Minton Regent shape (Plate 745). *G.A. Godden.*

Plate 747
TEA CUP. D 3⅝in (92mm) Ht 2½in (63mm).
Minton, the cup unmarked, the saucer bearing the Minton impressed year mark for 1862, designated as 'D, Regent Shape' in the Minton shape book, decorated with blue and gold stripes. *Dover Street Antiques, Canterbury, Kent.*

Plate 748
TEA CUP. D 3¾in (95mm) Ht 2in (50mm).
Minton and Boyle, blue printed 'Felspar' back stamp and pattern number 3428, fluted cup with rudimentary inner spur in the loop handle, decorated with a Worcester type blue ground pattern. *The Victoria & Albert Museum.*

Plate 749
TEA CUP. D 3⅝in (92mm) Ht 2¹⁄₁₆in (52mm).
Derby, Bloor period, crown and Gothic D mark, waisted cup decorated with a dark blue ground with reserved panels, enamelled flowers and elaborate gilding, kicked loop handle. *The Berthoud Collection.*

Plate 750
COFFEE CUP. D 2¹³⁄₁₆in (71mm) Ht 2⁹⁄₁₆in (64mm).
Derby, Bloor period, crown and Gothic D mark, straight sided thickly potted cup decorated with a grey ground with enamelled roses and gilt leaves, handle similar to that shown in Plate 749. *The Berthoud Collection.*

Plate 751
TEA CUP. D 3¾in (95mm) Ht 2⅛in (53mm).
Factory A, no mark, scallop edged bone china cup decorated with a blue transfer printed 'Broseley' pattern. *Philip Miller.*

Plate 752
TEA CUP. D 3⅝in (92mm) Ht 2½in (63mm).
Davenport, marked DAVENPORT in green, earthenware cup with scalloped edge decorated with an all over under glaze green printed pattern embellished with blue and pink enamel. *Private Collection.*

Plate 753
TEA CUP. D 3¾in (95mm) Ht 2¹/₁₆in (52mm).
Factory A, no mark, moulded and ribbed cup decorated inside with a gilt grape and vine pattern, the handle similar to those in Plates 697-702. *Philip Miller.*

Plate 754
COFFEE CUP. D 3⁵/₁₆in (84mm) Ht 2⅝in (66mm).
Factory A, no mark, cup matching that shown in Plate 753, (compare Plates 697-702). *Philip Miller.*

Plate 755
TEA CUP. D 3¹³/₁₆in (97mm) Ht 2⅛in (53mm).
Att. to G.F. Bowers imitating Rockingham, the saucer marked with the Rockingham griffin etched into the glaze and subsequently removed, pattern 2078, c. 1852, fluted cup with scalloped edge decorated with crude blue flowers on a grey ground. *Bruce Newmane.*

Plate 756
COFFEE CUP. D 3⅜in (86mm) Ht 2⁹/₁₆in (64mm).
Alcock, pattern number 4929 in red, strongly moulded cup with spiral ribbing, decorated inside with a dark blue ground, cartouches with yellow 'curlicue bar' (see Plate 787) and good quality gilding. *The Berthoud Collection.*

Plate 757
COFFEE CUP. D 3³⁄₁₆in (81mm) Ht 2¼in (56mm).
Davenport, puce crown mark 'Davenport, Longport' and pattern number 874, cup with moulded ribs and leaves, decorated with enamelled flowers and fine gilding. *The Berthoud Collection.*

Plate 758
COFFEE CUP. D 3³⁄₁₆in (81mm) Ht 2½in (63mm).
Davenport, brown wreath mark and pattern number 914, cup with moulded ribs and leaves, decorated with pink and yellow flower sprays. *Private Collection.*

Plate 759
TEA CUP. D 4³⁄₁₆in (106mm) Ht 2¼in (56mm).
Davenport, puce crown and 'Davenport, Longport, Staffordshire' and pattern number 901, with scalloped and moulded lip decorated with green leaves and gilding. *Private Collection.*

Plate 760
COFFEE CUP. D 3½in (89mm) Ht 2⁷⁄₁₆in (61mm).
Davenport, brown wreath mark, flared lip, and characteristic heavily potted handle, decorated with gilding only. *Private Collection.*

Plate 761
COFFEE CUP. D 3¹¹⁄₁₆in (94mm) Ht 2½in (63mm).
Davenport, brown wreath mark and pattern number 986, cup with moulded leaves round the flared lip, decorated with green leaf pattern and gilding. *Private Collection.*

Plate 762
COFFEE CUP. D 3¾in (95mm) Ht 2⅜in (60mm).
Davenport, blue seal mark usual on printed patterns and pattern number 1055, waisted bell shaped cup decorated with a blue printed pattern. *Private Collection.*

Plate 763
TEA CUP. D 4in (101mm) Ht 2³/₁₆in (55mm).
Hilditch & Hopwood, pattern number 2025, decorated with a buff ground and rococo panels with an enamelled rose in the centre, elaborate spur at the top (Helm (21) Shape A4) (compare Plate 764). *The Berthoud Collection.*

Plate 764
TEA CUP. D 4⅜in (111mm) Ht 2in (50mm).
Chamberlain, printed mark 'Chamberlain's Worcester, 155 New Bond Street, London', scallop edged cup with high D handle with top spur decorated inside with flower sprays and rather crude gilding. *Dr. Geoffrey & Alma Barnes Collection.*

Plate 765
TEA CUP. D 3¹³/₁₆in (81mm) Ht 2⅛in (53mm).
Grainger, no mark, gadrooned inner edge to a flared lip, decorated with enamelled birds in branches and vine leaves and grapes, the D handle smaller than in Plate 764. *The Berthoud Collection.*

Plate 766
COFFEE CUP. D 3³/₁₆in (81mm) Ht 2½in (63mm).
Grainger, pattern number 575, gadrooned inner edge to a flared lip, decorated inside and out with a crudely painted Imari pattern. *The Berthoud Collection.*

Plate 767
TEA CUP. D 3¾in (95mm) Ht 2¼in (56mm).
Factory unknown, net embossed cup with pedestal foot and two elaborate cartouches containing lilac sprigs, handle with three spurs. *The Berthoud Collection.*

Plate 768
COFFEE CUP. D 3⅛in (79mm) Ht 2¾in (69mm).
Probably Grainger, no mark, gadroon edged cup decorated inside with a blue ground, gilding and typical birds in panels, border of large shark's tooth gilding (compare Plates 765 and 766). *City Museum & Art Gallery, Stoke-on-Trent.*

Plate 769
TEA CUP. D 4¼in (107mm) Ht 2¼in (56mm).
Grainger, pattern number 1909x, moulded edge cup decorated inside with an enamelled bird in a circular landscape, typical ring and spur handle. *The Berthoud Collection.*

Plate 770
TEA CUP. D 4⅜in (111mm) Ht 2⁵⁄₁₆in (58mm).
Grainger, marked 'Grainger, Worcester, Moss Fibre', scallop edged cup of similar shape to that shown in Plate 769 but more heavily modelled, heavier handle. *The Berthoud Collection.*

Plate 771
TEA CUP. D 4¹⁄₁₆in (103mm) Ht 2³⁄₁₆in (55mm).
Grainger, no mark, moulded edge cup, this flower and bead border also used at the Coalport, Ridgway and Derby factories but only on dessert wares, decorated inside and out with a grey printed thistle pattern, ring and spur handle with small moulded flower (compare Plate 599). *The Berthoud Collection.*

Plate 772
TEA CUP. D 3¹¹⁄₁₆in (94mm) Ht 2¼in (56mm).
Factory unknown, ribbed and waisted cup with rather crude lustre decoration, handle similar to Grainger (Plates 598, 599 and 771) and Copeland & Garrett (Plate 600). *Jean Sewell Antiques.*

Plate 773
TEA CUP. D 4¼in (107mm) Ht 2¹⁄₁₆in (52mm).
Ridgway, crown mark in puce, wavy edged cup decorated inside with a green ground, white panels and enamelled birds in a tree, well modelled ring handle with a moulded flower on the thumb rest and large moulded upper attachment. *The Berthoud Collection.*

Plate 774
TEA CUP. D 4¹⁄₁₆in (103mm) Ht 2½in (63mm).
Zacchariah Boyle and Son, 1825-1850, the saucer with brown printed mark 'Vignette' and 'ZB&S', earthenware cup with brown printed pattern of leafy twigs inside and out and inside with a man offering a flower to a woman on horseback. *The Berthoud Collection.*

Plate 775
TEA CUP. D 4⅛ (104mm) Ht 2½in (63mm).
Factory unknown, no mark, scallop edged cup decorated inside and out with a grey printed pattern of birds and butterflies, moulded ring and spur handle, probably made at Coalport as a replacement for a Bowers service (see Plates 781, 791 and 816). *Philip Miller.*

Plate 776
TEA CUP. D3¹⁵⁄₁₆ (100mm) Ht 2⅜ (60mm).
Factory unknown, pattern number 819 in blue, moulded leaves and basket weave border, decorated with printed and enamelled flowers, moulded ring handle with outer spur. *Dr. Geoffrey & Alma Barnes Collection.*

Plate 777
TEA CUP. D 4⅜in (111mm) Ht 2⅛in (53mm).
Factory unknown, lobed edge cup decorated inside with a blue border and three yellow leaves, enamelled flowers in the centre, moulded ring handle with top spur, possibly Alcock or a replacement. *B. & A. Downes Antiques.*

Plate 778
TEA CUP. D 3¹⁵⁄₁₆in (100mm) Ht 2⅜in (60mm).
Factory unknown, no mark, lobed edge cup with a pedestal foot decorated inside with bluish green leaves and gilding, moulded ring and spur handle. *The Berthoud Collection.*

Plate 779
TEA CUP. D3¹⁵⁄₁₆ (100mm) Ht 2⅛in (53mm).
Factory unknown, pattern number 267, decorated with a sketchy landscape and gilding, ring handle with upper and lower spur. *Patricia Ratcliffe Antiques.*

Plate 780
TEA CUP. D3¹⁵⁄₁₆in (100mm) Ht 2¼in (56mm).
Factory unknown, no mark, scrolling leaf moulded border, decorated with crudely gilt bell flowers, ring handle with upper and lower spurs. *The Berthoud Collection.*

Plate 781
TEA CUP. D 4³/₁₆in (106mm) Ht 2⅛ (53mm).
Coalport, pattern number 2/896, moulded edge cup with ring and spur handle, the ring less rounded than that of Alcock (Plates 782 and 784) and the spur more upright than that of Davenport (Plate 783), decorated with enamelled flowers and with the moulding picked out in gilding. *The Berthoud Collection.*

Plate 782
TEA CUP. D 4¼in (107mm) Ht 2¹/₁₆in (52mm).
Alcock, pattern number 1/2183, slightly moulded edge, decorated with a drab band with a yellow edge and central enamel flower spray, rounder ring and spur handle than on Coalport cups (Plate 781). *The Berthoud Collection.*

Plate 783
TEA CUP. D 4¼in (107mm) Ht 2⅜in (60mm).
Davenport, puce crown mark and 'Davenport, Longport, Staffordshire', with ring and spur handle (compare with Coalport and Alcock, Plates 781, 782 and 784), decorated with a flown blue pattern, green enamel and gilding (see Lockett (6) Plate 84(iii)). *Private Collection.*

Plate 784
TEA CUP. D 2⅜in (60mm) Ht 1¼in (31mm).
Alcock, pattern number 6/4890, miniature cup decorated with a red and green border, with round ring and spur handle. *Philip Miller.*

Plate 785
TEA CUP. D 4⅛in (104mm) Ht 2¼in (56mm).
Factory unknown, pattern number 97, wavy edged cup decorated with a gilt pattern only, oval ring and spur handle (compare Plate 781). *D.R Pomfret.*

Plate 786
TEA CUP. D 4⅛in (104mm) Ht 2¼in (56mm).
Factory unknown, no mark, decorated with turquoise enamel panels and printed flowers, oval ring and spur handle. *D.R. Pomfret.*

Plate 787
TEA CUP. D 4in (101mm) Ht 2³/₁₆in (55mm).
Alcock, pattern number 5195, waisted pedestal cup with moulded edge, decorated inside with pale yellow leaves, hatched gilding and 'curlicue bar' outside, rustic open handle. *Philip Miller.*

Plate 788
COFFEE CUP. D 3¼in (82mm) Ht 2⅝in (66mm).
Alcock, pattern number 5588, moulded edge pedestal cup decorated with small maroon and yellow flowers, rustic open handle. *The Berthoud Collection.*

Plate 789
TEA CUP. D 4¼in (107mm) Ht 2⅛in (53mm).
Alcock, pattern number 5866 in red, moulded edge cup decorated with blue bars, central flower sprays and gilt barley ears, well modelled rustic 'bean' handle. *The Berthoud Collection.*

Plate 790
COFFEE CUP. D 3¾in (95mm) Ht 2¾in (69mm).
Alcock, pattern number 7345 in green, narrow waisted cup with pedestal foot and tooth moulded edge, decorated with red flowers and green leaves, crudely modelled rustic 'bean' handle. *The Berthoud Collection.*

Plate 791
TEA CUP. D 4³/₁₆in (106mm) Ht 2⅜in (60mm).
Alcock, no mark, pedestal cup with rustic 'bean' handle decorated with a Bowers' grey printed pattern, probably a replacement (compare Plate 775). *Philip Miller.*

Plate 792
TEA CUP. D 3⅜in (86mm) Ht 1⅝in (41mm).
Alcock, no mark, miniature tea cup decorated with a pink butterfly print inside and out, with rustic 'bean' handle. *The Berthoud Collection.*

Plate 793
TEA CUP. D 4¹/₁₆in (103mm) Ht 2in (50mm).
Minton, pattern number 1852W with slightly scalloped edge and ring handle with no thumb rest (compare Alcock's similar handle, Plate 795), decorated with a typical Minton pattern of flowers on an apricot ground. This shape appears in the Minton shape book as 'A, Blenheim', but the pattern numbers recorded suggest a date in the 1840s. *The Berthoud Collection.*

Plate 794
COFFEE CUP. D 3⁷/₁₆in (87mm) Ht 2½in (63mm).
Minton, pattern number 2095, with scalloped rim and ring handle shown in the Minton shape book as 'A, Blenheim', decorated with a blue band inside and enamelled flowers below the scalloped edge. *Christopher May.*

Plate 795
TEA CUP. D 4¹/₁₆in (103mm) Ht 2⅛in (53mm).
Alcock, pattern number 7918, slightly wavy edge cup decorated with pale drab and yellow panels and printed and enamelled flowers, plain oval ring handle. *Gus Brain Atiques.*

Plate 796
TEA CUP. D 4¹/₁₆in (103mm) Ht 2⅛in (53mm).
G.F. Bowers, pattern 652, wavy edged cup decorated with a maroon ground and yellow leaves, oval ring handle with flattened spur on the top. *The Berthoud Collection.*

Plate 797
TEA CUP. D 4⅛in (104mm) Ht 2¹/₁₆in (52mm).
Davenport, puce crown mark, and 'Davenport, Longport, Staffordshire', and pattern number 1411, scallop edged cup with ring handle and rudimentary spur decorated with dark blue leaves and gilding. *The Berthoud Collection.*

Plate 798
COFFEE CUP. D 3½in (89mm) Ht 2½in (63mm).
Davenport, puce crown mark and 'Davenport, Longport, Staffordshire' and pattern number 1320 with ring handle and rudimentary spur, decorated inside with grey panels, flower sprays and gilding. *Alan Townsend Collection.*

Plate 799
TEA CUP. D 4⅛in (104mm) Ht 2in (50mm).
Factory unknown, pattern number 884, moulded edge cup decorated inside with a drab ground colour and elaborate gilding, well painted flower spray in the centre, oval ring handle set low on the cup. *The Berthoud Collection.*

Plate 800
COFFEE CUP. D 3½in (89mm) Ht 2⅝in (66mm).
Alcock, pattern number 8184 in puce, cup with pedestal base, decorated inside with a green and pale yellow border and enamelled flowers, oval ring handle set well above the rim. *Philip Miller.*

Plate 801
TEA CUP. D 3¹/₁₆in (78mm) Ht 2½in (63mm).
Davenport, puce registration mark for 1845, cup with moulded sides decorated with an orange ground and gilding, oval ring handle set against the cup. *Private Collection.*

Plate 802
COFFEE CUP. D 2¹⁵/₁₆in (74mm) Ht 2¾in (69mm).
Spode, no mark, cup with slightly flared rim, decorated with a gilt pattern and the motto 'Spectemur Acendo' (from a regimental service), the oval ring handle with upper and lower supports but angled against the cup. *The Victoria & Albert Museum.*

Plate 803
TEA CUP. D 3⅝in (92mm) Ht 2in (50mm).
Minton, pattern number 4182, a slightly waisted cup with scalloped edge and distinctive ring handle with a thickened ridge or crest at the top, decorated with printed roses, leaves and birds (shown in the Minton shape book as 'S3'). *The Minton Factory Museum, Stoke-on-Trent.*

Plate 804
COFFEE CUP. D 2⁹/₁₆in (64mm) Ht 2½in (63mm).
Davenport, blue wreath mark and pattern number 1886, faceted cup with ring handle revived from c.1805, decorated with blue and yellow grounds and gilding. *Private Collection.*

Plate 805
COFFEE CUP. D 3in (76mm) Ht 2½in (63mm).
Copeland & Garrett, Felspar back stamp in green and pattern number 5189, melon shaped cup, a later version of Spode's 5146 shape with more thickly modelled handle and upper spur (compare Plate 697), decorated with a green ground and gilding. *City Museum & Art Gallery, Stoke-on-Trent.*

Plate 806
COFFEE CUP. D 2¹³⁄₁₆in (71mm) Ht 2½in (63mm).
Minton, marked M1603 only, with embossed scroll work enclosing a panel and latticed embossing, decorated with forget-me-not sprays, (designated 'I, Net Embossed' in the Minton shape book). *City Museum & Art Gallery, Stoke-on-Trent.*

Plate 807
TEA CUP. D 3¹⁵⁄₁₆in (100mm) Ht 2⅛in (53mm).
Factory unknown, applied blue pad mark in the shape of a twelve pointed star and 28, cup with moulded foot and a row of moulded flowers above, lilac floral and scroll sprigging, kicked handle with opposed spurs. *The Berthoud Collection.*

Plate 808
COFFEE CUP. D 3⁵⁄₁₆in (84mm) Ht 2⅜in (60mm).
Factory unknown, pattern number 1136 in red, cup with plain pedestal foot, decorated inside and out with a dark blue ground with embossed shells in yellow, handle similar to that shown in Plate 807. *Jean Sewell Antiques.*

Plate 809
COFFEE CUP. D 3¹⁄₁₆in (78mm) Ht 2⅜in (66mm).
Factory unknown, Sèvres mark in pale blue enamel, green ground pebbled with seeded gilding, cartouche containing enamelled flowers surrounded by raised gilding, deeply kicked handle with rudimentary top spur, badly spotted glaze inside. Possibly Madeley. *Jean Sewell Antiques.*

Plate 810
COFFEE CUP. D 3in (76mm) Ht 2⁹⁄₁₆in (64mm).
Factory unknown, pattern number 2483, cup with a band of moulded ribbing, twisted loop handle, decorated with a grey ground, landscapes and elaborate gilding (see Plate 676), possibly Hilditch. *Bill Dickenson, Ironbridge.*

Plate 811
TEA CUP. D 4in (101mm) Ht 2¼in (56mm).
G.F. Bowers, the saucer marked with a Staffordshire knot enclosing the letters GFB and the pattern name 'Fibre', of bone china decorated in black and gold. *The Berthoud Collection.*

Plate 812
TEA CUP. D 4in (101mm) Ht 2¼in (56mm).
G.F. Bowers, the saucer marked GFB and 'Dresden Wreath', pattern 473, moulded cup with a pair of embossed leaves, decorated with printed and enamelled flowers. *The Berthoud Collection.*

Plate 813
TEA CUP. D 3¹⁵/₁₆in (100mm) Ht 2in (50mm).
Att. to William Adams, no mark, shallow moulded cup with five pairs of ribs, decorated inside with an apricot ground, gilt vines and leaves, handle with vertical top spur. *City Museum & Art Gallery, Stoke-on-Trent. (Percy W.L. Adams Collection).*

Plate 814
COFFEE CUP. D 3⅛in (79mm) Ht 2½in (63mm).
Factory unknown, pattern number 3768 in grey, cup with ribbed moulding, slightly scalloped lip, decorated with enamelled floral pattern inside and out, handle with upper spur (compare Plate 813). *City Museum & Art Gallery, Stoke-on-Trent.*

Plate 815
TEA CUP. D 3⅞in (98mm) Ht 1¹⁵/₁₆in (49mm).
Factory unknown, pattern number 4417 in red, cup with five pairs of ribs, decorated inside with a dark blue ground and pale yellow leaves, good quality gilding with sprays of enamelled flowers (compare Plate 813). *Roy Hodges.*

Plate 816
TEA CUP. D 4in (101mm) Ht 2¼in (56mm).
G.F. Bowers, no mark, cup with pairs of moulded leaves, decorated with enamelled flower sprays of similar shape to that shown in Plate 812. *The Berthoud Collection.*

Plate 817
TEA CUP. D 4in (101mm) Ht 2⅜in (60mm).
Att. to H. & R. Daniel, pattern number 6379, six lobed cup with a band of moulded acanthus leaves above a slightly lobed pedestal base, decorated with green leaves and enamelled flowers, divided and entwined handle in the form of two snakes (compare Plate 818 and 819): *Beaubush House Antiques, Folkestone.*

Plate 818
TEA CUP. D 4in (101mm) Ht 2⅜in (60mm).
Coalport, marked 'Coalport, England, leadless glaze' (c. 1891-1920) of similar form to the cup shown in Plate 817 but with more pronounced lobe to the base and heavier handle, decorated inside and out in dark blue over a black transfer print (see Plates 559 and 560). *Clive House Museum, Shrewsbury.*

Plate 819
COFFEE CUP. D 3¼in (82mm) Ht 2¾in (69mm).
Att. to H. & R. Daniel, pattern number 8447, six lobed cup with a band of moulded acanthus leaves above a high pedestal base, entwined handle in the form of two snakes, simply decorated with dashes of grey and raised turquoise flowers. *The Berthoud Collection.*

Plate 820
TEA CUP. D 4in (101mm) Ht 2⅞in (72mm).
Att. to H. & R. Daniel, pattern number 8925, moulded edge cup on a high moulded pedestal, decorated with a maroon border with yellow scrolls and three small enamelled landscapes, elaborate gilding, high loop handle and divided upper attachment (pattern number 1/124 has been recorded). *The Berthoud Collection.*

Plate 821
TEA CUP. D 4⁵/₁₆in (109mm) Ht 2⅜in (60mm).
Ridgway, pattern number 7652 (c. 1840), 'Savoy' shape waisted cup on a high, lobed pedestal, loop handle with divided upper attachment, decorated with a blue border and yellow leaves (see Godden (16) Plate 97). *The Berthoud Collection.*

Plate 822
COFFEE CUP. D 3¹¹/₁₆in (94mm) Ht 2¹³/₁₆in (71mm).
Ridgway, pattern number 2/7790, 'Savoy' shape cup matching that shown in Plate 821, decorated with two bands of drab colour and a band of enamelled flowers. *The Berthoud Collection.*

Plate 823
TEA CUP. D 4⅛in (104mm) Ht 2⅝in (66mm).
Coalport, no mark, cup with slightly flared lip decorated with a blue printed pattern divided and entwined handle with leaf attachments above and below. *Bill Dickenson, Ironbridge.*

Plate 824
TEA CUP. D 3¼in (82mm) Ht 2in (50mm).
Coalport, no mark, shallow cup decorated with a blue printed pattern, entwined handle. *Clive House Museum, Shrewsbury.*

Plate 825
TEA CUP. D 3¾in (95mm) Ht 2⁵⁄₁₆in (58mm).
Coalport, pattern number 2/810 (c. 1830), slightly waisted cup with a turquoise blue ground and gilding, entwined handle. *Bill Dickenson, Ironbridge.*

Plate 826
TEA CUP. D 3⅝in (92mm) Ht 2⅜in (60mm).
Factory unknown, no mark, slightly waisted cup decorated with a rich blue band with enamelled flowers, entwined handle. *The Berthoud Collection.*

Plate 827
COFFEE CUP. D 3¼in (82mm) Ht 2½in (63mm).
Coalbrookdale, no mark, c. 1820, decorated with a turquoise ring and pink roses and gilding, entwined handle. *Bill Dickenson, Ironbridge.*

Plate 828
COFFEE CUP. D 3⅛in (79mm) Ht 2¹³⁄₁₆in (71mm).
Ridgway, pattern number 2/9436 (c. 1845), six lobed. slightly waisted cup with entwined handle (compare Plates 5 and 6), decorated with a drab ground and enamelled flowers. *The Berthoud Collection.*

Plate 829
TEA CUP. D 3⅜in (86mm) Ht 2⁷/₁₆in (61mm).
Worcester, Kerr & Binns period c. 1852-1862, no mark, waisted cup decorated with a Marbled White butterfly and grasses, entwined handle. *The Dyson Perrins Museum, Worcester.*

Plate 830
BREAKFAST CUP. D 3¹³/₁₆in (97mm) Ht 2½in (63mm).
Copeland, plain interlaced Cs mark, waisted cup with Sèvres type divided handle, decorated with a green floral printed pattern. *The Berthoud Collection.*

Plate 831
COFFEE CUP. D 3¼in (82mm) Ht 2½in (63mm).
Minton, unmarked, slightly waisted cup with entwined handle, decorated with under glaze prints of landscapes and flowers in bright green, designated in the Minton shape book as 'S' (no name given). *The Berthoud Collection.*

Plate 832
COFFEE CUP. D 2⁵/₁₆in (58mm) Ht 2³/₁₆in (55mm).
Minton, crown and globe mark and 'Minton's made for Mortlocks, Oxford Street' and pattern number 5089, small coffee cup with pineapple moulding and entwined handle, decorated with printed and enamelled flower sprays. *The Berthoud Collection.*

Plate 833
TEA CUP. D 3⅞in (98mm) Ht 2⁹/₁₆in (64mm).
Minton, pattern number A7401, a straight sided cup with entwined handle shown in the Minton shape book as shape 'W', decorated with two bands of turquoise blue, a thin pink line and gilt meandering leaf pattern. *The Berthoud Collection.*

Plate 834
TEA CUP. D 3⁹/₁₆in (90mm) Ht 2in (50mm).
Minton, with back stamp including 'Minton' and 'English Porcelain Depot, VS Paris', and pattern number G569 of flattened Bute shape with entwined handle shown in the Minton shape book as 'S2', decorated with printed and enamelled flowers on a scale ground. *The Berthoud Collection.*

Plate 835
TEA CUP. D 3⅛in (79mm) Ht 2in (50mm).
Factory unknown, pattern 99 (in gold on the saucer) shallow ribbed cup on a pedestal base decorated with floral lilac sprigging on the outside and a Large Copper butterfly and landscape inside, well modelled handle. *Private Collection.*

Plate 836
TEA CUP. D 3⅝in (92mm) Ht 2⅛in (53mm).
Factory unknown, marked with a crown and H & B and registered number 135869 c. 1899 (Godden (15) gives three firms with these initials but none working at this date), decorated with an inky blue pattern inside and out, poorly modelled handle. *Private Collection.*

Plate 837
TEA CUP. D 3⅞in (98mm) Ht 2³⁄₁₆in (55mm).
Factory unknown, pattern 467 (on the saucer) ribbed cup on a pedestal base decorated inside with roses and a tulip and with pink lustre. *The Berthoud Collection.*

Plate 838
COFFEE CUP. D 3⅛in (79mm) Ht 2¼in (56mm).
Factory unknown, pattern number 349, well modelled cup with twenty vertical flutes decorated with enamelled flowers inside. *Philip Miller.*

Plate 839
TEA CUP. D 3⅝in (92mm) Ht 2⅛in (53mm).
Factory unknown, no mark, cup 'made in the 1930's to supply gaps in a New Hall service' but in a shape not usually associated with that factory, decorated inside with enamelled flowers. *The City Museum & Art Gallery, Stoke-on-Trent.*

Plate 840
TEA CUP. D 3⅝in (92mm) Ht 2in (50mm).
Royal Stafford China, crown mark and England, c. 1912, decorated with an orange print and coloured enamels. *Bill Dickenson, Ironbridge.*

Plate 841
BREAKFAST CUP. D 3¾in (95mm) Ht 3¾in (95mm).
Rockingham/Baguley, griffin mark partly obscured by the glaze, c.
1842-1846, cup of plain shape decorated with a thick brown 'treacle'
glaze,gilded oval ring handle with horizontal spur. *Bruce Newmane.*

Plate 842
BREAKFAST CUP. D 3¹⁵/₁₆in (100mm) Ht 3in (76mm).
Davenport, blue wreath mark and pattern number 2604, revived
Bute shape cup with ring handle and thumb rest, decorated with an
on-glaze printed pattern of pink roses and green leaves. *The Berthoud
Collection.*

Plate 843
BREAKFAST CUP. D 4⁷/₁₆in (113mm) Ht 2¾in (69mm).
Minton, the saucer with impressed 'Mintons' and the year mark for
1874 and pattern number G3567, revived Bute shape with embossed
swags and some gilding. *City Museum & Art Gallery, Stoke-on-Trent.*

Plate 844
TEA CUP. D 3½in (89mm) Ht 2⅜in (60mm).
Alcock, pattern 1/3513, moulded cup with eight pairs of ribs
decorated with blue panels, yellow roses and gilding, plain loop
handle. *Dr. Geoffrey & Alma Barnes Collection.*

Plate 845
BREAKFAST CUP. D 3⅝in (92mm) Ht 2⅞in (72mm).
Grainger, shield mark c. 1870-1889, straight sided cup decorated
with a blue leaf pattern, plain loop handle. *Bill Dickenson, Ironbridge.*

Plate 846
TEA CUP. D 3⅛in (79mm) Ht 2½in (63mm).
Grainger, marked 'Grainger & Co. Manufacturers, Worcester and 24
Princess Street, Manchester' c. 1860, straight sided cup decorated
with a dark blue ground with combed gilding, plain loop handle. *Gus
Brain Antiques.*

Plate 847
TEA CUP. D 3⅛in (79mm) Ht 2⁹⁄₁₆in (64mm).
Derby, puce baton and SH mark c. 1870, straight sided cup decorated with an elaborate gilt pattern with raised blue spots and triple enamelled roses, well modelled loop handle with opposing spurs. *The Berthoud Collection.*

Plate 848
COFFEE CUP. D 3¼in (82mm) Ht 2½in (63mm).
Factory unknown, pattern number 2513 in red, straight sided cup with very elaborate gilding on a claret ground with touches of pale yellow and green, ring handle with two spurs. *The Berthoud Collection.*

Plate 849
COFFEE CUP. D 3¼in (82mm) Ht 2⁹⁄₁₆in (64mm).
Hilditch & Hopwood, pattern number 2222, moulded cup decorated with a fawn ground and gilding, broken loop handle. *Philip Miller.*

Plate 850
TEA CUP. D 3³⁄₁₆in (81mm) Ht 2½in (63mm).
Hilditch & Hopwood, no mark, cup with slightly flared lip decorated with a pink border and enamelled flowers, loop handle with two spurs. *D.R. Pomfret.*

Plate 851
TEA CUP. D 3½in (89mm) Ht 2⅝in (66mm).
Davenport, blue wreath mark and pattern number 557, of Bute shape with a loop handle with rudimentary thumb rest and inner spur, decorated with an orange border and gilding. *Private Collection.*

Plate 852
COFFEE CUP. D 2⁹⁄₁₆in (64mm) Ht 2⅜in (60mm).
Baguley, Mexborough, the saucer marked 'Rockingham Works, Mexborough, Baguley' in a garter, straight sided cup decorated with a thick brown 'treacle' glaze. (Rice (18) records that after the death of Isaac Baguley in 1865 his son removed the factory to Mexborough.) *Private Collection.*

Plate 853
COFFEE CUP. D 3⁷/₁₆in (87m) Ht 3in (76mm).
Ridgway, no mark, cup with slightly flared lip, decorated with an orange ground with landscapes and gilt swags in reserved panels, well modelled handle. *Dr. Geoffrey & Alma Barnes Collection.*

Plate 854
TEA CUP. D 3⅛in (79mm) Ht 2¼in (56mm).
Davenport, orange crown mark and 'Davenport, Longport, Staffordshire' and pattern number 3545, revived Bute shape with reinforced loop handle, decorated with a rich Imari pattern. *Private Collection.*

Plate 855
TEA CUP. D 3⅝in (92mm) Ht 2¹¹/₁₆in (68mm).
Ridgway, no mark, presentation documentary cup with diaper moulded base above a pedestal foot, decorated with a claret ground with apricot panels and gilding. On the front 'Presented to Mr. Charles Rhodes', on the back 'By John Ridgway & Co. 1853'. *G.A. Godden.*

Plate 856
TEA CUP. D 3¹³/₁₆in (97mm) Ht 2⁵/₁₆in (58mm).
George Jones, Crescent China mark (c. 1924-1951) spiral moulded cup with raised leaves emphasised by the gilding, reinforced loop handle. *Bill Dickenson, Ironbridge.*

Plate 857
CABINET CUP. D 2¹³/₁₆in (71mm) Ht 2⅝in (66mm).
Worcester, Kerr & Binns period c. 1852-1862, no mark, two handled cabinet cup decorated with a medallion portrait of a child and with swags and ribbons in green and gold. *The Dyson Perrins Museum, Worcester.*

Plate 858
COFFEE CUP. D 2⅝in (66mm) Ht 2⅞in (72mm).
Minton, pattern number C461, pedestal footed cup decorated with a turquoise band and enamelled flowers, graceful ring handle. *The Berthoud Collection.*

Plate 859
COFFEE CAN. D 2¹¹/₁₆in (68mm) Ht 2¹¹/₁₆ (68mm).
Davenport, marked with a crown and 'Davenport, Longport, Staffordshire' in orange and pattern number 2615, tapered coffee can decorated with a blue and orange Imari pattern enriched with gilding. *Mona & Gerald Sattin.*

Plate 860
COFFEE CUP. D 2⅜in (60mm) Ht 2¼in (56mm).
Davenport, no mark, earthenware cup decorated with a mauve printed pattern, reinforced ring handle. *The Berthoud Collection.*

Plate 861
COFFEE CUP. D 3¹/₁₆in (78mm) Ht 2¹¹/₁₆in (68mm).
Davenport, pattern number 2845, cup with slightly flared lip, the lower two thirds with ribbed moulding, decorated with an orange ground and a continuous band of gilt oak leaves, handle with slight thickening at the top. *Private Collection.*

Plate 862
COFFEE CAN. D 2¼in (56mm) Ht 2⅛in (53mm).
Davenport, marked 'Davenport, Longport, Staffordshire' and pattern number 2075, late coffee can decorated with an orange and blue Imari pattern and with the loop handle in a ridged and knopped form. *Gus Brain Antiques.*

Plate 863
COFFEE CUP. D 3⅛in (79mm) Ht 2¾in (69mm).
Davenport, blue wreath mark and pattern number 3164, cup with slightly flared lip, decorated with a green chain pattern, loop handle. *Private Collection.*

Plate 864
COFFEE CUP. D 3in (76mm) Ht 2¾in (69mm).
Davenport, crown mark and 'Davenport, Longport, Staffordshire' and pattern number 3246 with plain loop handle, decorated with a ground of gold stars and panels of enamelled flowers. *Private Collection.*

Plate 865
CABINET CUP. D 2¹⁵⁄₁₆in (74mm) Ht 2¹³⁄₁₆in (71mm).
Worcester, Kerr & Binns period, uncrowned circle mark c. 1852-1862, honeycomb pierced cup decorated with barbeaux sprigs, turquoise bands and gilding, bamboo moulded handle. *The Dyson Perrins Museum, Worcester.*

Plate 866
CABINET CUP. D 2¹¹⁄₁₆in (68mm) Ht 2½in (63mm).
Grainger, no mark, floral pierced cabinet cup on a pedestal base, the flowers decorated with blue and apricot and with green leaves, gilded handle. *The Dyson Perrins Museum, Worcester.*

Plate 867
COFFEE CUP. D 3¹⁄₁₆in (78mm) Ht 2¹¹⁄₁₆in (68mm).
Worcester, Kerr & Binns period, uncrowned circle mark, waisted cup with Sèvres type spiral moulded base, decorated with a panel of pale blue lines and gilding. *The Victoria & Albert Museum.*

Plate 868
COFFEE CUP. D 3¹⁄₁₆in (78mm) Ht 2⁹⁄₁₆in (64mm).
Grainger, pattern number 2/1507, pedestal footed cup decorated with green flowers on a paler green ground and gilding, reinforced loop handle. *The Dyson Perrins Museum, Worcester.*

Plate 869
COFFEE CUP. D 2¾in (69mm) Ht 2¾in (69mm).
Grainger, marked 'Grainger & Co., Manufacturers Worcester' and pattern number 2/805, decorated with a turquoise band and gilding and with a strongly reinforced handle. *Gus Brain Antiques.*

Plate 870
TEA CUP. D 3½in (89mm) Ht 2⁷⁄₁₆in (61mm).
Royal Worcester, printed shield mark for 1902, cup with flared lip decorated with a blue and gold border, complex spurred handle. *Dover Street Antiques, Canterbury.*

Plate 871
TEA CUP. D 3³/₁₆in (81mm) Ht 1¹⁵/₁₆in (49mm).
Copeland, marked 'Copeland's China' and pattern number 6102, faceted cup shanked from left to right with scalloped rim, decorated with an orange printed pattern and dusted gilding. The cup dates from c. 1860 and suggests that a new series of pattern numbers had by then been introduced. *The Berthoud Collection.*

Plate 872
COFFEE CUP. D 3¹/₁₆in (78mm) Ht 2⅝in (66mm).
Copeland, decorated interlaced C's mark and pattern number 8261, quatrefoil cup with slightly scalloped rim, c. 1850-1860, decorated with a thick on-glaze orange ground with gilt renaissance scroll design. *The Berthoud Collection.*

Plate 873
BREAKFAST CUP. D 4⅛in (104mm) Ht 2¾in (69mm).
Copeland, decorated interlaced Cs mark and pattern number 1/1183, Bute shape cup decorated with a blue ground, white flowers and gilding, leaf moulding on top of the loop handle. *Christopher May.*

Plate 874
TEA CUP. D 3⅝in (92mm) Ht 1¾in (44mm).
Cauldon, marked 'Cauldon England' c. 1905-1920 (successors to Ridgway and Brown-Westhead & Moore), eggshell thin cup decorated with a rich blue ground and gilt border, plain loop handle. *The Berthoud Collection.*

Plate 875
TEA CUP. D 3⁵/₁₆in (84mm) Ht 2⅛in (53mm).
Minton, made for Thomas Goode, London, shallow cup decorated with a raised gold and platinum pattern of plums and leaves, butterflies and beetles. *Roy Hodges.*

Plate 876
TEA CUP. D 3¾in (95mm) Ht 1¾in (44mm).
Cauldon, marked 'Cauldon, England' and pattern number 2253, c. 1905-1920 (successors to Ridgway and Brown-Westhead & Moore), shallow lobed cup decorated with pink roses and gilding, scroll handle in the Ridgway tradition (compare Plate 615). *Giulia Irving.*

Plate 877
TEA CUP. D 3³/₁₆in (81mm) Ht 2½in (63mm).
Sir James Duke and Nephews (Hill Pottery, formerly S. Alcock & Co.) impressed hand mark on the saucer, pattern number 5/4692 on the cup and 6/7336 on the saucer, decorated with blue vine leaves and grey flowers, typical pebble gilding, handle with top spur. *The Victoria & Albert Museum.*

Plate 878
COFFEE CUP. D 3in (76mm) Ht 2¾in (69mm).
Att. to Alcock, pattern number 1/2467 in pink, cup with moulded panels, decorated with a branch and berry pattern in maroon and pale yellow with 'elder twig' gilding, broken loop handle with blunt double spur on the top. *Private Collection.*

Plate 879
COFFEE CUP. D 3¼in (82mm) Ht 2⅝in (66mm).
Att. to Alcock, pattern number 1/6437, slightly ribbed cup decorated with a pale fawn ground and green leaves and with an enamelled bird in a tree and pink ribbon, loop handle with top spur. *Private Collection.*

Plate 880
COFFEE CUP. D 2¾in (69mm) Ht 2¾in (69mm).
Att to Alcock, pattern number 4/503, decorated with a blue ground with yellow panels, typical pebble gilding (compare Plate 877), reinforced handle with single spur. *City Museum & Art Gallery, Stoke-on-Trent.*

Plate 881
COFFEE CUP. D 3⁷/₁₆in (87mm) Ht 2¾in (69mm).
Att. to Alcock, pattern number 615 in gold, slightly ribbed body and moulded border, decorated with a maroon ground with yellow leaves and typical pebble gilding, loop handle. *The Berthoud Collection.*

Plate 882
COFFEE CUP. D 2¹³/₁₆in (71mm) Ht 2⅝in (66mm).
Att. to Alcock, pattern number 6/6453, cup with slightly flared lip, decorated with a maroon ground, pale buff and white leaves, loop handle. *Liz Jackson Antiques.*

Plate 883
COFFEE CUP. D 3⅜in (86mm) Ht 2⅜in (60mm).
William Adams, pattern number 9 on the saucer, from a service partly marked with an impressed wreathed anchor, slightly ribbed moulding, decorated with gilding only, moulded loop handle. *D.R. Pomfret.*

Plate 884
COFFEE CUP. D 2⅞in (72mm) Ht 2⅝in (66mm).
Factory unknown, pattern number 133 in red, decorated with drab panels and swags of flowers, kicked loop handle. *Private Collection.*

Plate 885
TEA CUP. D 3¾in (95mm) Ht 2⅜in (60mm).
Factory unknown, pattern number 2/566, moulded cup with pairs of flutes curled at the top, decorated with a green border and enamelled rose in the centre, badly formed ring handle. *Bill Dickenson, Ironbridge.*

Plate 886
COFFEE CUP. D 3³⁄₁₆in (81mm) Ht 2¾in (69mm).
Factory unknown, pattern number 2/566, cup matching that shown in Plate 885. *Bill Dickenson, Ironbridge.*

Plate 887
COFFEE CUP. D 3⅝in (92mm) Ht 2⅜in (60mm).
Factory unknown, no mark, cup with flared lip decorated with a chinoiserie pattern in orange and gold, small ring handle with top spur. *Philip Miller.*

Plate 888
COFFEE CUP. D 3in (76mm) Ht 2⁹⁄₁₆in (64mm).
Factory unknown, pattern number 1/3934 in blue, plain unmoulded cup, simple border pattern of gold and blue with pink roses, broken ring handle with three spurs. *Private Collection.*

Plate 889
TEA CUP. D 4⅞in (123mm) Ht 1¾in (44mm).
Belleek, registered mark for 1872 and 3, very shallow moulded cup with a pearly glaze on three feet, decorated with a dark brown and pink band, square handle. *Dover Street Antiques, Canterbury.*

Plate 890
COFFEE CAN. D 2⁷⁄₁₆in (61mm) Ht 2¼in (56mm).
Minton, unmarked, with a square handle, decorated with a printed pattern of ruins and the legend 'A Gift from the Potteries'. *The Minton Factory Museum, Stoke-on-Trent.*

Plate 891
TEA CUP. D 3³⁄₁₆in (81mm) Ht 2⅛in (53mm).
Minton, marked 'Minton Delft, England' and pattern number G1613 of bucket shape, decorated with a blue printed floral pattern, square handle. *The Berthoud Collection.*

Plate 892
TEA CUP. D 3⅛in (79mm) Ht 2¼in (56mm).
Factory unknown, marked 'TEB BM' and registered mark c. 1884, of bucket shape decorated with a maroon print of birds in a tree, square handle. *The Berthoud Collection.*

Plate 893
TEA CUP. D 3¼in (82mm) Ht 2⅛in (53mm).
Coalport, pattern number 7/946 on the saucer, waisted cup decorated with a blue band, raised white enamelled beads, square stepped handle. *Doremy Antiques, Herne Bay, Kent.*

Plate 894
TEA CUP. D 3³⁄₁₆in (81mm) Ht 2¼in (56mm).
Coalport, standard crown mark c. 1881-1891, quatrefoil cup with a printed pattern of birds and bamboo in a solid gold ground, compressed loop handle. *Clive House Museum, Shrewsbury.*

Plate 895
COFFEE CUP. D 2¾in (69mm) Ht 2½in (63mm).
Royal Worcester, year mark for 1884 and pattern number 733 in red, straight sided cup with reinforced ring handle, decorated with a brown printed border. *Dover Street Antiques, Canterbury.*

Plate 896
COFFEE CUP. D 2¹⁵/₁₆in (74mm) Ht 2¾in (69mm).
Royal Worcester, pattern number 6099/2, straight sided cup decorated with an enamelled pattern of birds and ivy leaves, rustic handle. *Private Collection.*

Plate 897
TEA CUP. D 3½in (89mm) Ht 2¹/₁₆in (52mm).
Grainger, pattern number 2/1, shallow cup on a pedestal foot decorated with enamelled flowers on a pale blue ground, handle in the shape of a 'small G'. *The Dyson Perrins Museum, Worcester.*

Plate 898
COFFEE CUP. D 2⅝in (66mm) Ht 2⅜in 60mm).
Minton, registered mark for 1868 and pattern number A7657, bucket shaped coffee cup with a green and brown rustic handle with moulded ivy leaves on the cup. *Private Collection.*

Plate 899
COFFEE CUP. D 2¾in (69mm) Ht 2¹¹/₁₆in (68mm).
Bodley, pattern number 7/3481 and Bodley impressed on the saucer, straight sided cup decorated with green leaves and grey flowers on a cream ground, plain loop handle. *The Berthoud Collection.*

Plate 900
COFFEE CUP. D 3¹³/₁₆in (97mm) Ht 2¾in (69mm).
Goss, Goshawk mark and 'WH Goss, Cottage Pottery', oatmeal coloured earthenware cup with flared lip, decorated with enamelled hollyhocks and motto 'Droon yer sorrows'. *Private Collection.*

Plate 901
TEA CUP. D 3½in (89mm) Ht 2¼in (56mm).
Coalport, crown mark and 'Coalport Bone China, Made in England', shanked moulding with twisted loop handle, a blander version of an earlier moulding, undecorated except for the gilt handle. *The Berthoud Collection.*

Plate 902
TEA CUP. D 3⅜in (86mm) Ht 2in (50mm).
Minton, pattern number 2157, moulded cup decorated with a lavender ground and gilt rustic handle, moulded oak leaves and acorn feet. *Beaubush House Antiques, Folkestone.*

Plate 903
TEA CUP. D 3½in (89mm) Ht 2³/₁₆in (55mm).
Booth's brown printed Peacock mark and pattern number 20 in black, post 1891, earthenware cup decorated with a blue ground with gilt birds and panels of flowers. *Private Collection.*

Plate 904
COFFEE CUP. D 3in (76mm) Ht 2⁹/₁₆in (64mm).
Belleek, black printed mark, post 1891, cup with a pearly glaze and embossed grasses decorated in natural colours, divided rustic handle. *Private Collection.*

Plate 905
TEA CUP. D 3⁹/₁₆in (90mm) Ht 2⁵/₁₆in (58mm).
Brown-Westhead & Moore, registered mark for 1882, pedestal footed cup decorated with a maroon ground with flowers and gilding, gilt moulded rope handle. *City Museum & Art Gallery, Stoke-on-Trent.*

Plate 906
CUSTARD CUP. D 2⅞in (72mm) Ht 2¾in (69mm).
Worcester, Kerr & Binns period c. 1852-1862, pedestal cup decorated with enamelled birds and butterflies and a gilt B, green band with raised gilding, ring handle. *The Dyson Perrins Museum, Worcester.*

BIBLIOGRAPHY

(1) Henry Sandon, *The Illustrated Guide to Worcester Porcelain 1751-1793*

(2) G.A. Godden, *A Problem Class of Eighteenth Century English Porcelain Part I and II, The Collector's Guide June and July 1979*

(3) David Holgate, *New Hall and Its Imitators*

(4) G.A. Godden, *Caughley and Worcester Porcelains 1775-1800*

(5) H.G. Bradley, *Ceramics of Derbyshire 1750-1975*

(6) T.A. Lockett, *Davenport Pottery and Porcelain 1794-1887*

(7) Leonard Whiter, *Spode*

(8) Reginald Haggar and Elizabeth Adams, *Mason Porcelain and Ironstone 1796-1853*

(9) G.A. Godden, *Coalport and Coalbrookdale Porcelains*

(10) G.A. Godden, *Godden's Guide to Mason's China and the Ironstone Wares*

(11) Pat Halfpenny and Terry Lockett, *Staffordshire Porcelain 1740-1851, a Catalogue of the Third Exhibition of the Northern Ceramics Society 1979*

(12) John Cushion, *Pottery and Porcelain Table Wares*

(13) G.A. Godden, *An Illustrated Encyclopedia of British Pottery and Porcelain*

(14) Alan Smith, *The Illustrated Guide to Liverpool Herculaneum Pottery*

(15) G.A. Godden, *The Encyclopedia of British Pottery and Porcelain Marks*

(16) G.A. Godden, *The Illustrated Guide to Ridgway Porcelain*

(17) M.E. Berthoud, *H. & R. Daniel 1822-1846*

(18) D.G. Rice, *The Illustrated Guide to Rockingham Pottery and Porcelain*

(19) W.D. John, *Nantgarw Porcelain*

(20) R.G. Haggar and Wolf Mankowitz, *The Concise Encyclopedia of English Pottery and Porcelain*

(21) P.R. Helm, *Phoenix Rising; An Introduction to Hilditch,* article in the *Northern Ceramics Society Journal 1975/1976*

(22) T.A. Lockett, *Minton in 1810,* article in the *Northern Ceramics Society Journal 1980/1981*

(23) W.D. John, *Swansea Porcelain*

INDEX

Unidentified (*continued*)

400, 401, 402, 405, 406, 407, 408, 417, 443, 444, 459, 460, 461, 462, 472, 477, 478, 480, 482, 494, 500, 508, 516, 517, 518, 519, 521, 522, 523, 524, 528, 537, 538, 543, 545, 546, 580, 581, 587, 588, 590, 591, 592, 596, 606, 607, 614, 616, 618, 626, 627, 628, 629, 630, 635, 638, 639, 640, 641, 642, 649, 650, 651, 652, 653, 654, 658, 660, 664, 666, 668, 676, 713, 714, 736, 737, 741, 742, 755, 767, 768, 772, 775, 776, 777, 778, 779, 780, 785, 786, 799, 807, 808, 809, 810, 814, 815, 826, 835, 836, 837, 838, 839, 848, 877, 878, 879, 880, 881, 882, 884, 885, 886, 887, 888, 892

W(xxx)

Plates 247, 248

Wedgwood

Plates 177, 178, 179, 180, 185, 253, 329, 330, 466

Wood, Enoch

Plates 733, 735

Worcester

Plates 1, 6, 7, 8, 9, 12, 25, 26, 37, 39, 40, 42, 43, 51, 55, 65, 90, 115, 116, 151, 277, 278, 280, 281, 282, 301, 302, 303, 304, 305, 306, 339, 340, 435, 505, 506, 557, 829, 857, 865, 867, 870, 895, 896, 906